DICTIONARY

AND
PRONUNCIATION
GUIDE

Jan O'Meara

Illustrations by Jamie Bollenbach

ISBN: 0-9621543-0-X

Wizard Works
P.O. Box 1125
Homer, Alaska 99603

DICTIONARY

and Pronunciation Guide

INTRODUCTION

Every area has its own jargon and slang — language formed out of its past and modified by its people, language that separates the insider from the outsider. Alaska is no different from any other place in that regard, but its unique blend of cultures and lifestyles — Eskimo, Indian, Russian, American, prospector, trapper, logger, fisherman, oilman, homesteader — has given it a richly colorful and imaginative language.

This book is intended to give the newcomer and visitor the information they need to understand many of the words and phrases they will come across while in Alaska. It is not comprehensive, but contains the most common expressions readers may encounter.

Sounds ring differently on different ears, so some people may not agree with my pronunciation guide, but it reflects the way I have heard the words sounded over the years.

Words included in some definitions that are explained more fully elsewhere are entered in all capital letters.

Pronunciation Key

a = the short a, as in hat

ah = the short o, as in hot and hard

aw = the drawn out o, as in gone and lawn

ay = the long a, as in hay, hey, or weigh

e = the short e, as in fed

ee = the long e, as in feed and easy

i = the short i, as in hit

y = the long i, as in why and line

o = the long o, as in go

oo = the long u, as in boot

yoo = the diphthong heard in cute and mute

u = the medium u, as in put and foot

uh = the short u, as in cut and above

ow = the diphthong heard in how, cloud, and sauerkraut

s = the soft s, as in surf

z = the hard s, as in deserve

f = the breathy f, as in off

v = the buzzy f, as in of and love

A

ADAK (ay' dak) — Aleutian island and U.S. Navy base. The original military installation was an airfield built in just 10 days in September of 1942, during the Aleutian campaign of World War II. The 28-mile-long island was named by Russian fur hunters, perhaps, it is said, after the **ALEUT** word "adaq," or feather.

AERIAL TRAPPING — Hunting wolves by aircraft, then landing and shooting them; formerly one of the officially sanctioned methods for trapping wolves. In 1988 it was banned, but was replaced by airborne hunting, which allows basically the same thing. Both are opposed by **CONSERVATIONISTS**, who oppose the killing of wolves in general.

A.F.N. — Alaska Federation of Natives; political organization formed in 1967 by Alaska's disparate Native groups to pursue settlement of their land claims against the federal government. In the 1980s it again represented **NATIVE** interests and lobbied to get Congress to amend certain provisions of the **ALASKA NATIVE CLAIMS SETTLEMENT ACT** scheduled to take effect in 1991. At the same time, some Natives — particularly those pushing for **SOVEREIGNTY** — became disenchanted with the organization, saying it didn't truly represent their interests. While it has remained active in federal politics, state politics are usually handled by the **BUSH CAUCUS**.

AFOGNAK (uh fawg' nak) — Mountainous island north of **KODIAK**, second largest island in the Kodiak group; home of Alaska's only herd of Roosevelt Elk, which started with a transplant of eight animls in 1920 and reached a peak population of 1,500 in the mid 1960s. A village of the same name and located on the island was totally destroyed in the **GOOD FRIDAY EARTHQUAKE** of 1964 and the residents moved to the village of Port Lions on Kodiak.

AG LAND — Short term for agricultural land, land owned by the state and either leased or sold for agricultural purposes only, with the state retaining the SUBSURFACE RIGHTS and all other rights to the use of the land. It is one way to let people use the land without losing its agricultural potential. Agriculture in Alaska includes horticulture, tree farming, hay cutting, and livestock grazing.

ALASCOM (uh las' kahm) — Alaska's major long distance telephone service provider; took over the Alaska Communications Systems network from the U.S. Air Force in 1971; caught by deregulation in the late 1980s in a battle for market supremacy.

ALASKA DAY — October 18 holiday that celebrates the transfer of Alaska from Russian to U.S. ownership. In SITKA, site of the transfer ceremonies, residents mark the day with parades, parties, and period costumes. The United States purchased the RUSSIAN AMERICA colony in 1867 for $7.2 million, in a steal of a deal arranged by Secretary of State William H. Seward. Opponents of the purchase called it Seward's Folly and referred to the northern territory as Seward's Ice Box, but Alaska's wealth of minerals, timber, fish and physical beauty have long since justified Seward's judgment.

ALASKA NATIVE BROTHERHOOD — NATIVE rights organization founded by the TLINGIT Indians in 1912 to fight for the right of Alaska Natives to vote and hold office in the territory and the right to compensation for loss of their land; forerunner to the A.F.N.

ALASKA NATIVE CLAIMS SETTLEMENT ACT — Act passed by Congress in 1971, providing for the payment to Alaska's Natives of $965.2 million and 40 million acres of land. Most of the money and the land passed to regional and village corporations set up under the act to provide a source of continuing income for the Natives. Only NATIVES who registered by an established deadline could participate in the settlement and hold shares in the corporation. Passage of the act resolved immediate ownership claims and cleared the way for Congressional approval of the trans-Alaska oil pipeline project, which brought **PRUDHOE BAY** oil to U.S. markets.

ALASKA TUXEDO — Slack and jacket ensemble of wool whipcord, somewhat resembling a heavy-duty leisure suit; de rigueur dress for Alaskan social gatherings, becoming archaic in cosmopolitan circles but very much in evidence where real Alaskans gather; also sometimes called the **BUSH** tuxedo.

ALASKAN HIGH KICK — Event in the **WORLD ESKIMO INDIAN OLYMPICS** that looks as difficult as it is; the competitor sits on the floor, grabs one foot with the opposite hand, places the other hand on the floor, and tries to kick a suspended seal skin ball with the free foot; the record is 6'8''.

ALCAN (al' kan') — Popular name of the Alaska Highway, which runs 1,520 miles from Dawson Creek, British Columbia, Canada, to **FAIRBANKS**. The highway was hacked out of woods, rocks, and **MUSKEG** in about eight months during World War II, under agreement with Canada, and provided the first all-land access to Alaska from the **LOWER 48**. The Canadian section was turned over to Canada at the end of the war. Until recently, most of the Canadian section was gravel, providing inspiration for a popular bumper sticker: "I drove the Alaska Highway and survived."

ALEUT (al' ee oot') — Indigenous population of the **ALEUTIAN ISLANDS**; one of Alaska's major **NATIVE** groups. Subjugated by Russian fur hunters in the 18th century, they went from an estimated population of 15,000-30,000 to about 2,500 in about 100 years, in the process losing their independence, their culture, and their names. Most Aleuts today bear Russian surnames.

ALEUTIAN (uh loo' shuhn) **ISLANDS** — Chain of islands that stretch more than 1,000 miles from the tip of the Alaska

AMCHITKA

PENINSULA to the western **BERING** Sea; site of the **THOUSAND MILE WAR**, the only World War II campaign to be fought on American soil. The more than 200 islands are treeless, windswept, and frequently fogbound. Also called the Aleutian Chain or just the **CHAIN**.

ALPENGLOW (al' puhn glo') — Warm winter light that turns fields, forests and mountain tops a rosy pink, notable in Alaska particularly from late fall to early spring when sunrise comes late and sunset early, but also observable on mountaintops in the middle of the night in midsummer; a lighting feature predominant on many paintings of Alaska's snowclad mountains.

ALYESKA (al ee es' kuh) — (1) One of Alaska's original names, an **ALEUT** word meaning "the great land," which originally referred to the Alaska **PENINSULA**; (2) a popular ski resort south of **ANCHORAGE**, named for 3,939-foot-high Mount Alyeska.

AMCHITKA (am chit' kuh) — Aleutian island used by the U.S. military as an airbase in World War II and by the Atomic Energy Commission for underground nuclear tests in 1971. The latter use sparked some opposition from people concerned about nuclear testing in general and about its possible impact on the island's population of sea otters. Many of the otters were moved and transplanted to other coastal areas of Alaska and California as a result of the furor their possible demise caused.

ANCHORAGE (ank' er ij) — Alaska's largest city, containing about half the people in the state; began life in 1915 as a tent city during construction of the Alaska Railroad, now hub of much of the state's economic activity. Most of the livelihood of the city's more than 200,000 residents comes from federal, state or municipal government, oil, or one of the service industries; there is little industry here. The city has become so urbanized, it is sometimes described as being "only a half-hour from Alaska."

ANCHORAGE

ANCHOR POINT — Small community of about 1,500 people on the **KENAI PENINSULA** south of Anchorage on the shores of **COOK INLET**, named for a nearby point which was given the name by Capt. James Cook after he reportedly lost an anchor there. It lies adjacent to the Anchor River, a popular **SALMON** and **STEELHEAD** stream.

ANCSA (ank' suh) — Acronym for the **ALASKA NATIVE CLAIMS SETTLEMENT ACT.**

ANILCA (uh nil' kuh) — Acronym for the Alaska National Interest Lands Conservation Act, adopted by Congress in 1980, which set aside more than 100 million acres for **WILDLIFE REFUGES**, national monuments, and recreation areas. The act was an offshoot of the **ALASKA NATIVE CLAIMS SETTLEMENT ACT**, and the lands affected by it were also called **D-2 LANDS** for the paragraph in the earlier act that enabled the withdrawal. Lands selected under **ANILCA** and **ANCSA** are not subject to state selection under the statehood act, which gave the state government 104 million of Alaska's 375 million acres.

ANWR (an' wahr) — Acronym for **ARCTIC NATIONAL WILDLIFE REFUGE.**

AQUACULTURE — Fish farming; an attempt to enhance and perpetuate the commercial **SALMON** fishing industry in Alaska by raising fish from egg to **FRY** and then releasing the immature fish into Alaskan waters so they can imprint on the area, swim out to sea to grow to be big fish, and return either to be caught by fishermen or to **SPAWN** and thereby produce more fish. A more controversial method, opposed by many commercial fishermen, involves pen-rearing fish to salable size, such as is done in some European countries.

ARCTIC (ark' tik or ar' tik) — The area in Alaska above 66 degrees north latitude, ranging from the Brooks Range on the south, clear to the North Pole; often used to describe winter conditions in other areas of Alaska as well (as in arctic night, arctic wind, or arctic cold). The arctic differs from Antarctica in that it is not all ice and snow, but only looks that way in winter, when everything freezes.

ARCTIC NATIONAL WILDLIFE REFUGE — 18-million-acre wildlife refuge in the northeast corner of Alaska, best known as the calving grounds of the Porcupine **CARIBOU** herd, and focus of controversy in the late 1980s over the wisdom of opening the **REFUGE** to oil exploration and development.

ATHABASKAN (ath' uh bas' kuhn) — Also spelled Athabascan and Athapaskan; one of Alaska's major Indian groups, whose territory covers most of Alaska's **INTERIOR**, from north of the **ARCTIC** Circle to **COOK INLET** on the south and from Canada, west almost to the **BERING** Sea. Nomadic and semi-nomadic hunters originally, they developed the **SNOWSHOE** and the birchbark canoe. Most now live in permanent villages, but still rely on **SUBSISTENCE** hunting for their livelihood. They are renowned for their beadwork, which can be found in museums and gift shops all across the state. Athabaskan is a linguistic, rather than ethnic, distinction. There were 11 different Athabaskan languages in Alaska, and related languages are found in northwest Canada and the American southwest.

AUGUSTINE (aw' guh steen) — Short name for **MOUNT AUGUSTINE VOLCANO.**

AUKE (awk) BAY — Suburb of **JUNEAU** and docking point for the **SOUTHEAST** Alaska **STATE FERRY**, which is part of the state's **MARINE HIGHWAY** System.

AURORA BOREALIS (au ror' uh bor ee al' is) — Spectacular light show in Alaska winter skies, ranging in shape from sheets to waves and in color from red to green, caused by solar electrons striking gas particles in Earth's upper atmosphere; a common feature found in many paintings of Alaskan winters, difficult to capture on canvas and almost impossible to capture on film. Some people claim to be able to hear the lights crackle on still nights. Also called the **NORTHERN LIGHTS** or just plain aurora. The Southern Hemisphere enjoys a similar phenomenon, called the aurora australis.

AVALANCHE (a' vuh lanch) — Snow slide of large proportion, often containing enough force to uproot trees and carry along huge boulders; a hazard for skiers and other winter sports enthusiasts, and for motorists on roads below steep slopes; occur most frequently in early spring, during prolonged winter warming trends, or when there has been a heavy wet snowfall. Avalanche control consists of setting them off purposely, usually with some type of loud noise such as an explosion. Still, they can occur unexpectedly, and the highway between **ANCHORAGE** and the **KENAI PENINSULA** is often closed for hours in the winter until they can be cleared.

AVALANCHE CHUTE — The path an avalanche travels, often year after year; a wide swath down a hillside that looks like it was cut by a mad **CAT SKINNER** and is lined with broken trees.

B

BALEEN (bay' leen) — Fringed plates that line the mouths of baleen whales (as opposed to toothed whales) and during feeding filter out fish and tiny shrimp-like organisms called krill; a by-product of commercial and subsistence whaling, formerly used by Europeans and Americans for corset stays and buggy

THE U.S. PARK SERVICE
AVALANCHE CONTROL
PROGRAM.

whips, now used by some Alaska **NATIVES** for handcrafted items to be sold to tourists and other collectors of Alaskan art. Baleen whales include the blue, fin, right, **BOWHEAD**, gray, **HUMP-BACK** and the minke (mink' ee). The great Moby Dick of literary and cinematic fame was not a baleen whale but a toothed whale.

BANANA BELT — Area of Alaska that is warmed by Pacific currents, especially coastal **SOUTHCENTRAL** Alaska and **SOUTHEAST** Alaska, so called because it's an area of relatively warm winters, compared to the rigors of **INTERIOR** temperatures. It's not uncommon for winter temperatures in the Banana Belt to rise above freezing, sometimes into the 40s or 50s, bringing rain instead of snow, and it's rare for temperatures to dip below minus 35 degrees Fahrenheit. Ironically, the state's warmest summer temperatures are not in this zone, but in the interior, which in winter may suffer temperatures colder than minus 60 degrees Fahrenheit.

BANYA (ban' yuh) — **NATIVE** steambath used for cleansing, relaxing, and for curing aches and pains and other physical woes; usually consists of a small, low, log and sod cabin.

BARABARA (buh rah' buh ruh) — Semi-subterranean houses of the aboriginal **ALEUTS**, built mostly of sod and driftwood. Because they were partially underground, they did a better job of keeping the warmth in and the cold out than traditional frame housing. The earliest Russian hunters adopted the same style of housing. Now entirely outmoded and supplanted by Western-style housing. The Russians also called **DENA'INA** houses barabaras, although they were built differently than the Aleut homes.

BARANOF (bayr' uh nof or buh rah' nov) ALEX-ANDER — First governor of the **RUSSIAN AMERICA** colony and manager of the Russian-America Company. He served his company and country in Alaska for nearly 30 years, from 1791 to 1818, when he was replaced by a succession of governors, none of whom served more than five years in the colonies. He expanded the Russian Empire by moving the colony's headquarters from KODIAK to SITKA and sending colonists as far south as California. He greeted honored visitors to Sitka in formal attire — complete with a wig he tied on with a scarf — and entertained them at lavish dinners, during which he tried, usually successfully, to drink them under the table. Although he had a wife in Siberia, he fathered two children by the daughter of a NATIVE chief. The daughter of this union married the man who succeeded him as governor. Within months of his replacement, Baranof died of fever aboard ship while on his way back to Russia.

BARN DOOR — Slang term for extremely large HALIBUT, generally those larger than 200 pounds; sometimes also called a SOAKER.

BARREL STOVE — Wood and coal burning stove constructed from an empty 55-gallon fuel drum, found mostly in rural Alaska. Thousands of drums, also called "tundra daisies," were abandoned in rural Alaska following World War II and early oil exploration.

BARROW (bayr' o) — Farthest north community in Alaska, resting on the coast of the ARCTIC Ocean, about 1,300 miles south of the North Pole and nearly 1,000 miles north of ANCHORAGE. It gets the most and the least of Alaska's sun: for 84 days in the summer the sun never sets, and for 67 days in the winter it never rises. Low winter average temperature is minus 18 degrees Fahrenheit; high summer average is 39 degrees. The community of nearly 3,000 people is the seat of the 88,000-square-mile North Slope BOROUGH. Its original name, "Ikpeagvik," meant "place where owls are hunted."

BARTLETT, E.L. "BOB" — Territorial delegate to the U.S. Congress from 1944-1958 and one of the state's first senators after STATEHOOD. He served as senator until his death in 1968 following heart surgery. Alaskan attorney Ted Stevens was appointed

by then Gov. Walter **HICKEL** to replace him. An **ANCHORAGE** high school and an Alaska **STATE FERRY** is named after him.

BASKET — (1) Traditional artifact produced by **NATIVE** women and woven from grass or roots or made by folding and sewing birchbark; (2) ring of leather or plastic attached near the end of a ski pole to keep the pole from sinking into the snow; (3) bed and semi-enclosed portion of a dog sled. Teams competing in some dog sled races must cross the finish line intact, and dogs that can't make it on their own four feet are brought in in the basket.

BAY — Body of water that cuts into the land from an even larger body of water, that is no longer than it is wide and is at least a mile wide. There are many bays in Alaska, but the two most famous are **BRISTOL BAY** and **KACHEMAK BAY**.

BEAR — Alaska's most awe-, fear-, and story-inspiring mammal. Some people love them, some hate them, but all respect them. Alaska has three kinds of bears: big, bigger and biggest. The smallest, and the one that adapts most easily to human activity, is the black bear (**Ursus Americanus**), which may also be brown or cinnamon in color and even, rarely, blue-gray (called a glacier bear). It is distinguished from its larger cousins by size, shape and color — it has no hump at its shoulder, its nose slopes straight down from its brow, and it only reaches 200-300 pounds in size.

Brown bears (**Ursus horribilus**) are sometimes called dish-faced bears, for the concave shape of their profile. They are also called Kodiak bears and grizzlies. The only difference between a grizzly and another brown bear is the color — grizzlies have blonde guard hairs — although grizzlies are not usually seen in coastal areas. Brown bears are the real monsters of Alaska and the stuff of which myths are made. They have been known to reach 7-10 feet in height (standing on their hind legs) and 1,500 pounds in weight, and to run as fast as 35 miles an hour. Fortunately, they tend to be shy of people, and hikers often sing or carry noisemakers on the trail to advertise their presence. They are found throughout most of Alaska.

BEAR

Polar bears (**Thalarctos maritimus**) are huge bears with white coats. They inhabit Alaska's **ARCTIC** regions, and weigh 1,500 pounds or more. For years, they were one of Alaska's prime trophy animals for both their size and fur. In 1972, Congress banned hunting of polar bears and other marine mammals by anyone other than Alaska **NATIVES** who are **SUBSISTENCE** hunting. Other hunters and guides have supported the state government's sporadic efforts to gain control of **MARINE MAMMAL** management, hoping to end the hunting ban.

The males of all species of bear in Alaska are called **BOARS**, the females **SOWS**, and the young **CUBS**. Sows give birth to one or more cubs during hibernation and remain with them for one to three years. Although generally considered carnivores, bears are really omnivores — or perhaps a better word would be opportunists. They eat what is available, and relish berries and vegetation; sometimes in summer they can be seen grazing in meadows and on hillsides.

BEAR PAWS — Rather stubby type of **SNOWSHOE**, rounded on both ends, said to be preferable to more traditional shapes for use on hilly, open terrain.

BEAUFORT (bo' furt) SEA — Section of Arctic Ocean on Alaska's northeast and Canada's northwest coast, named in 1826 by English explorer Sir John **FRANKLIN** for a fellow officer; site of offshore oil leases north of the **NORTH SLOPE** and **PRUDHOE BAY**.

BELUGA (buh loo' guh) — Small, white, toothed whale (**Delphinapterus leucas**) often seen fishing along the Alaska coastline, particularly along **TURNAGAIN** Arm, where they chase **SALMON** and eulachon (see **HOOLIGAN**). They travel in groups, called pods, and have been called the canaries of the sea because of their chatter. They eat fish, squid and marine invertebrates, usually swallowing them whole. They average 16 feet in length, and can grow as large as 21 feet. The name is sometimes spelled ''belugha'' to distinguish it from the white sturgeon of Siberia, which is also called beluga.

BERING, VITUS (bayr' ing, vy' tuhs or vee' tus) —
Danish leader of the expedition which "discovered" Alaska for
Russia in 1741. Although he is credited for the discovery, there is
some evidence that earlier sailors also sighted Alaska. He never
enjoyed the fruits of his discovery, or even set foot on Alaskan soil,
for he died shipwrecked on an island in Siberian waters on his way
home. His men eventually made their way back to Siberia and
made a foretune selling the sea otter pelts they had gathered during the winter, setting the stage for more than 100 years of ex-
ploitation of Alaska's fur resources. Namesake of the Bering Sea
and Bering Straits.

BETHEL (beth' uhl) — Community of about 3,000 people
located in the Kuskokwim River delta in western Alaska; named
by Moravian missionaries after a biblical verse, Gen. 35:1 —
"And God said unto Jacob, arise, and go up to Bethel, and dwell
there, and make there an altar unto god...."

B.I.A. — Bureau of Indian Affairs, federal agency which ran
educational and health programs for rural Alaska NATIVES from
1931 until those duties were transferred to the state or to other
federal agencies. The state now has jurisdiction over schools, and
the U.S. Public Health Service manages the medical program.

BIDARKA, BAIDARKA (bi dar' kuh or bi dar' kee) —
Skin boat made and used by the ALEUTS, similar in shape and
style to the ESKIMO KAYAK; a narrow boat, pointed at both
ends, completely enclosed by skin except for a hole where the
boatman sat; used for both hunting and transportation. The
larger, open-style, family boat was called a baidar (by' dar) by
the Aleuts and an UMIAK by the Eskimos. Europeans who saw
the Aleuts bobbing along in the water in their bidarkas said they
appeared almost amphibious.

BILLIKIN (bil' i kin) — Pointy-headed, pot-bellied, grinning
good luck charm produced for the tourist trade by Alaska

ESKIMOS, following a design originally patented, it is said, in 1908 by a Kansas City woman and sold as good luck charms in Seattle during the 1909 Alaska-Yukon-Pacific Exposition.

BLACK GOLD — Oil, so named for the large profits reaped by successful developers of oil deposits and those who own the rights to the oil. In 1969, Alaska almost overnight went from being one of the poorest states in the union to being one of the richest when it sold a tract of oil leases at **PRUDHOE BAY** for $900 million plus royalties.

BLACK ICE — Dangerously deceptive winter road condition that consists of a totally smooth, nearly invisible, layer of ice. It and its cousin, **GLARE ICE**, have sent scores of surprised Alaskan motorists off the road and into the ditch over the years.

BLANKET TOSS — ESKIMO game in which a circle of people hold a walrus hide taut and toss a person standing on it into the air; the "tossee" can continue to jump as long as he or she can remain upright. Some say the maneuver was originally used to help hunters spot game, others say it was never more than a way to have fun. It is a featured event in the **WORLD ESKIMO INDIAN OLYMPICS**.

B.L.M. — Bureau of Land Management, the federal agency responsible for managing much of the federal land in Alaska. Other managers of federal land include the U.S. Forest Service, U.S. Park Service and U.S. **FISH AND WILDLIFE** Service. Although federal agencies manage much of the land in Alaska, the state manages all animals except **MARINE MAMMALS** and migratory birds, which has led to some conflict about hunting and trapping of animals located on game refuges.

BLUBBER — Fat of whales, walruses and other sea mammals, rendered into oil for lubricants and lighting by whalers but often enjoyed raw by Alaskan ESKIMOS (see MUKTUK). For the

BLANKET TOSS

Eskimos, the fat serves the same purposes as it did for the sea mammals: it keeps them warm, but in a different way. Blubber provides a tremendous number of calories per pound of food; the metabolic energy produced by consuming the fat keeps them warm. For sea mammals, the blubber acts as insulation.

BOAR — Male **BEAR**.

BOOTIES — (1) Protective foot coverings for sled dogs that are running in icy or mixed slush and ice conditions, particularly those entered in the **IDITAROD** Sled Dog Race; (2) down- or fiber-filled socks or slippers worn in winter camps or in the house to keep toes warm when the temperature drops.

BORE TIDE — A rushing, one- to six-foot high wall of water produced when a strong incoming tide surges into the constricted channel of an inlet; most pronounced where the tidal range is great, as it is in **COOK INLET**, where it reaches nearly 40 feet. The only regularly occurring bore tides are reported to be in **TUR-NAGAIN** and **KNIK** Arms of Cook Inlet, where they are visible twice a day, usually about two hours after the designated low tide in **ANCHORAGE**.

BOROUGH (bur' o) — The major unit of local government in Alaska, similar to counties in other states, having the power to tax personal and private property and the responsibility to run public schools. The services they provide depend on the type of borough and on the wishes of the local electorate. Some boroughs operate hospitals and offer fire protection and road maintenance. Some don't offer anything but education, which all boroughs are mandated by law to provide. There are 11 boroughs in Alaska, the largest being the 88,000-square-mile **NORTH SLOPE** Borough, the smallest being those which encompass a single city — such as the Municipality of **ANCHORAGE**, the City and Borough of **JUNEAU**, and the City and borough of **SITKA**. Other boroughs are the Fairbanks North Star Borough, Kodiak Island Borough, Kenai Peninsula Borough, Bristol Bay Borough, Ketchikan Gateway Borough,

Haines Borough, and Matanuska-Susitna Borough. The next rung down on the governmental ladder is the incorporated city, which provides many of the services the borough doesn't.

BOTTOMFISH — Generic name for the several species of fish that live along the sea bottom and are gathered by the tens of thousands of tons by commercial trawling operations. It is a fairly recent fishery for American fishermen, but one that has grown rapidly in recent years. Bottomfish harvests in Alaska went from 10,000 metric tons in 1980 to over 300,000 metric tons in 1987. The four mainstays of the fishery are pollock, Pacific cod, black cod, and rockfish. Some say bottomfishing is going to save the Alaska fishing industry. Others say it is going to wipe out species that sea mammals and sea birds need to survive.

BOWHEAD (bo' hed) WHALE — Large BALEEN whale hunted by Bering and BEAUFORT SEA ESKIMOS for SUB-SISTENCE, and a source of controversy between the NATIVES and the International Whaling Commission and those who are opposed to whaling in general. Natives say unrealistically low hunting quotas threaten their livelihood, but those on the other side fear that too high a quota and wasted kills (animals struck and lost) threaten what they believe is an already endangered species. There are an estimated 2,000-plus bowhead whales; the highest Eskimo harvest in recorded times was in 1976, with 48 and an additional 35 struck and lost; immediately after that, the whaling commission set a quota of 12, which has risen in recent years. The issue is sometimes used as a bargaining chip during commission deliberations, to encourage Japan to reduce or end its whaling activities.

BREAK-UP — Annual spring occurrence that signals the end of winter and the beginning of summer, brings ankle- and hub-deep mud to dirt roads and uncovers an unsightly accumulation of trash and automobile hulks formerly hidden under snow; the best antidote for CABIN FEVER and prevention for the SPENARD DIVORCE; what happens to relationships overtaxed by isolation and long winter nights; a good excuse to gamble (see NENANA ICE CLASSIC).

BRISTOL BAY — One of Alaska's richest fishing areas, lying off the west coast, above the Alaska **PENINSULA**; an area that produces about 20 percent of all **SALMON** caught in Alaskan waters each year and about 60 percent of the **SOCKEYE**; focus of a controversy in the 1970s and 80s over the potential economic benefits and environmental problems posed by a proposed federal oil lease sale in the area.

BROWNIE — Brown **BEAR**.

BULL — The male of several Alaska animal species, including **MOOSE**, **CARIBOU**, walrus, seals, and whales. The females are called **COWS** and the young are called **CALVES**, or in the case of seals, pups.

BULL COOK — Combination janitor, caretaker, handyman, and cook's helper in remote construction or timber camps.

BUNNY BOOTS — Oversize white, insulated rubber boots that keep one's feet from freezing but make them appear easily twice their normal size; said to be effective at temperatures well below minus 20 degrees Fahrenheit; so called because Alaska's "bunny," the **ARCTIC** hare, is white in the winter and has large hind feet — although a bunny with feet this big would be a big bunny indeed; now being replaced in some areas by **SHOE PACS** and **SORELS**.

BUSH — As in bush plane and bush pilot, but not to be equated with bush league — the Alaska equivalent of the Australian Outback; the area of Alaska that is not connected by road to the rest of Alaska, i.e., the majority of the state; rural Alaska. Bush pilots have opened up Alaskan communications and transportation by flying anywhere and everywhere in the state, landing their light planes on lakes, sand bars, glaciers, beaches and anywhere else they can find a flat surface. The only way most people have of getting into most of Alaska is by bush plane and the state is said to have more small planes per capita than anywhere else in the world.

BUSH CAUCUS — Coalition of Alaska NATIVE politicians that wields a great deal of influence in the state Legislature and tries to ensure that Native interests are not sacrificed to the will of the majority; a lump in the craw of party politicians.

BUOY (boo' ee or bo' ee) — Moored float used either to indicate the location of crab pots or as a navigational aid to mark passable channels. Navigational buoys are a specific size and shape and are tended by the U.S. Coast Guard. Fishing buoys range from commercially produced round **FLOATS** to plastic bleach bottles.

C

CABIN FEVER — Peculiar malady that grips Alaskans in mid-winter, described as a 12-foot stare in a 10-foot room; symptoms include increased irritability, often to the point of irrationality, and an insatiable appetite for the sun; without treatment it can lead to another Alaska phenomenon, the **SPENARD DIVORCE**; cured by three weeks in Hawaii or Mexico, or failing that by three weeks of rabble-rousing and near riot over some irrelevant issue; disappears with **GREEN-UP**.

CACHE (kash) — Little cabin on stilts, used for storing food out of reach of marauding animals; in general, a stash of food, supplies, or other valuables.

CALVE (kav) — To give birth to an offspring, used in referring to ungulates such as **MOOSE, REINDEER** and **CARIBOU** and sea mammals such as whales and walrus; also refers to the breaking off of large sheets or chunks of ice from **GLACIERS**; as a noun in plural form, refers to two or more young of the species listed above, the singular form is calf.

CAMP ROBBER — Canada jay, also called grey jay and **WHISKEY JACK**; medium-sized grey and white bird that has the brass and insatiable greed of an animal easily ten times its size. The nickname comes from their propensity for visiting campsites and taking as much of whatever they can find as they can get away with. They stash their ill-gotten gains and will return to the campsite again and again to fill their beaks to overflowing as long as the goodies remain. There is little they don't like, and they have even been known to pick dog dishes dry.

CANDLEFISH — Another name for **HOOLIGAN**, or eulachon, a small oily fish that can be eaten or burned as a candle.

CANNERY — Any plant that processes fish for later consumption, whether by freezing or canning; replaced the oldtime **SALTRY**. Before oil development, canneries controlled much of Alaska's economy and in some areas they are still the major seasonal employers.

CARIBOU (kayr' uh boo) — Alaska's indigenous **REINDEER**, which cluster in nomadic herds and inhabit most of the state. They are smaller than **MOOSE**, ranging in size from 175-400 pounds, and both sexes bear antlers that occasionally reach lengths of four feet.

CAT SKINNER — Slang term for a Caterpillar tractor driver, most often employed in Alaska on large-scale clearing or construction projects.

CANDLEFISH
(ALSO "ZIPPOFISH")

CHAIN — Shortened version of the **ALEUTIAN** Chain, refers to the islands as a whole.

CHEECHAKO (chee chaw' ko) — A newcomer to Alaska, as contrasted with a **SOURDOUGH**; in other areas called a greenhorn or tenderfoot; in any group, the one who sits wide-eyed and terrified while oldtimers haul out every scary bear story they know.

CHICKEN — (1)Small town in central eastern Alaska, near the Canadian border, on the road to Dawson City, said to be named for the **PTARMIGAN**, which early residents called a chicken; (2) a small **HALIBUT** of 10 to 20 pounds, so called because of their excellent taste; (3) what one feels like after coming across a gigantic brown **BEAR** track in the middle of a hiking path miles from the nearest help or haven.

CHILKAT (chil' kat) — (1)A subgroup of the **TLINGIT** Indians of **SOUTHEAST** Alaska that reside near **HAINES** and **SKAGWAY** at the head of the Lynn Canal; (2) the river valley north of Haines that is the winter gathering place for North America's largest concentration of bald eagles; (3) a particular style of woven dancing blanket noted for bold stylization and pattern; (4) another pass used by gold seekers to get to **INTERIOR** Alaska and the **KLONDIKE**, now traversed by the Haines Highway.

CHILKOOT PASS/TRAIL — Path trodden by thousands of eager prospectors on their way to the **KLONDIKE** gold fields in 1897-98; climbs from sea level at the head of the Lynn Canal to 3,739 feet and ends at Lake Bennett, Yukon Territory. During the peak of the **GOLD RUSH** an unbroken chain of gold-seekers spanned the trail from the foot of the mountain to the top of the pass. Most of them made the trip up and back several times to get all their gear from the bottom to the top. The average minimum gear was a ton a person, which meant 20 big trips. At Lake Bennett, voyagers built barges and boats to carry them northward. More than 1,500 hikers now climb the trail each year.

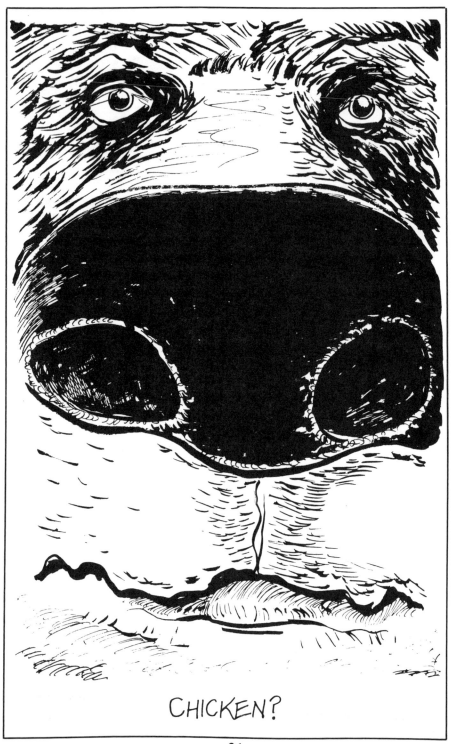

CHICKEN?

CHINOOK (shi nook') — (1)A warm wind that blows no ill, unless it is accompanied by rain in the winter (see **GLARE ICE**); (2) another name for one of Alaska's most popular sport and commercial fish, the **KING** salmon, which averages 11-30 pounds but has weighed in at 125 pounds.

CHIRIKOF (cheer' i kov) LT. ALEXEI — Commander of the second vessel in **BERING**'s 1741-42 expedition. He sailed his ship to **SOUTHEAST** Alaska, where he lost some of his men under mysterious circumstances. He sent a small boat ashore on one of the islands to gather water. When it did not return, he sent another boatful of men to find out what had happened. It disappeared too. Chirikov went back to Russia, and the Indians of Southeast Alaska didn't have to worry about Russians for another 40 years, but the "landfall" established Russia's claims to the area later.

CHITINA (chit' nuh) — Tiny community in the Copper River Valley northeast of **VALDEZ**, established in 1908 as a railroad stop on the Copper River and Northwestern Railway and as a supply town for the Kennecott Copper Mines at McCarthy. The mine and the railroad were abandoned in 1938 and the town became a ghost town, but in the 1970s and 80s it became modestly repopulated, growing to about 40 people.

CHUGACH (choo' gatch) — (1)A subgroup of **ESKIMOS** residing along the **GULF COAST** from the tip of the **KENAI PENINSULA** past **PRINCE WILLIAM SOUND**; (2) one of Alaska's 12 **NATIVE REGIONAL CORPORATIONS**; (3)state park on the outskirts of **ANCHORAGE**; (4)national forest that rims Anchorage and extends to Prince William Sound and the upper Kenai Peninsula; (5)coastal range of mountains that extends from Anchorage east almost to the Canadian border; (6)an electric company. Not to be confused with Chugiak (choo' gee ak), the community north of Anchorage.

CHUM — (1)Another of Alaska's five species of salmon, also called **DOG SALMON**, marketed primarily as canned salmon; (2)

CHUMS

cut up fish used as bait for more desirable species; (3) as a verb, to throw cut up fish or shrimp overboard to attract salmon or other types of fish.

CHUTE (shoot) — (1)Starting line and take-off area for sled dog races; (2) the path taken by an **AVALANCHE**.

CLAM — Succulent marine bivalve, gathered along beaches at low tide for both personal and commercial use. Of Alaska's approximately 160 species, the most popular are **RAZOR CLAMS**, cockles, and butter clams. Cockles and butter clams are the easiest to gather because they have short necks and have to stay near the surface. One has to work to get a razor, which has a long neck. You have to find a dimple in the sand, quickly dig down between the dimple and the sea to expose the clam, then drop to all fours and try to grab it by its neck before it gets away. Razors can be incredibly quick. **NATIVES** perfected a method of pinning the clam, by shoving a pencil width stick into the dimple and through the clam; then they could dig it out at their leisure. Although they are good eating, clams can also cause paralytic shellfish poisoning, said to be 1,000 times more potent than cyanide, and should only be gathered at approved beaches. Check with the Alaska Dept. of Fish and Game.

CLAN — A subdivision of **SOUTHEAST** Alaska and **ATHABASKAN NATIVE** groups. In **TLINGIT** and **HAIDA** tribes, the clans are named for various wildlife species. Major divisions are the Raven and Eagle or Wolf; subdivisions include the killer whale, frog, bear, beaver and other animals.

CLEAR-CUTTING — Wide-scale logging practice that clears a whole section of forest by cutting down all the trees in the area. It is a controversial practice. Proponents say it is the most economical way to harvest **TIMBER**; opponents say it leads to soil erosion and stream pollution and creates an eye-sore.

COHO (ko' ho) — Another of Alaska's popular sport and com-

THE SENSELESS TRAGEDY OF DRINKING AND CLEAR CUTTING.

mercial **SALMON**; also called silver salmon; a good-eating, hard-fighting fish that averages 6-12 pounds but feels like more on the end of a fishing line.

COLUMBIA GLACIER — Large **GLACIER** that spills into **PRINCE WILLIAM SOUND** west of **VALDEZ**. It used to be a regular stop for the Alaska **STATE FERRY** that connects the communities of **WHITTIER**, Valdez and **CORDOVA**. The ferry would blast its horn to try to make the glacier **CALVE** to give passengers a show. Charter boats from Valdez did the same thing. Eventually, so much ice was falling off, eroding the glacier and creating potential hazards for oil tanker traffic, the practice was discontinued.

CONSERVATIONIST — Depending on who's doing the telling: (a) anyone who wants to stop development and inhibit Alaska's economic growth, (b) anyone who wants to keep Alaska from being destroyed by greed, or (c) anyone who wants to align themselves with those who love Alaska's wildlife and scenery. Sometimes used as a compliment, sometimes as a pejorative. See also **DEVELOPER** and **PRESERVATIONIST**.

COOK INLET — A 200-mile-long **INLET** that extends from the Gulf of Alaska south of **HOMER** to the Susitna Flats north of **ANCHORAGE**, extended on the north by **KNIK** Arm and on the east by **TURNAGAIN** Arm; originally called Cook's River then Cook's Inlet, for Captain James Cook, who explored the area in 1778 on his third round-the-world voyage for England. He was killed later in the journey by natives in the Hawaiian Islands.

CORDOVA (kor do' vuh) — Small fishing community of about 2,000 people on the shores of **PRINCE WILLIAM SOUND** southeast of **VALDEZ**; former copper and coal shipping port. Like Valdez, its name reflects the Spanish presence in Alaska during the early days of exploration.

CORE SAMPLE — Sample of sedimentary layers taken during mineral exploration, after earlier exploration efforts have already indicated the possible presence of valuable minerals, used to determine the actual presence of oil and the size and grade of the find.

CORK — (1)**FLOAT** that holds up fishing nets, originally made of cork but now usually made of synthetic material; (2) tool for smoothing wax onto cross-country skis, also originally made of cork but now replaced by styrofoam; (3) as a verb, to cut another vessel off from the fish, or to fish very close to another boat or its gear.

CORN SNOW — Snow that has melted then re-frozen into clusters of tiny ice balls; forms a firm, fairly decent surface for skiing.

COW — Female of several Alaska mammals, including **MOOSE**, **CARIBOU**, seals, walrus, and whales.

CRITICAL HABITAT — Protective designation that restricts development and other activities that might be harmful to one or more important fish or game species in a particular area; usually recommended by **FISH AND GAME** and established by the state Legislature; similar in concept to **WILDLIFE REFUGE**.

CUB — Immature **BEAR**.

D

DALL (dahl) — Species of wild, white, big horned sheep that

DULL SHEEP

inhabit Alaska; usually seen in clusters in high mountain valleys as dots on the hillside, although they occasionally come down to roadside; named for William H. Dall, the scientist who first identified them in the late 1860s.

DALTON HIGHWAY — Formerly the **NORTH SLOPE HAUL ROAD**, built in 1974 to supply the **PRUDHOE BAY** oil field, turned over to the state in 1978. Only the first 211 miles are open to the public year round.

DAWSON — Short for Dawson City, the Yukon Territory boom town that arose during the **KLONDIKE GOLD RUSH** and is still a popular tourist attraction. Now a community of about 1,400 people, in its heyday Dawson served 30,000 residents. Not to be confused with Dawson Creek, the southern starting point for the **ALCAN** Highway.

DELTA BARLEY PROJECT — State-subsidized agricultural project centered southeast of **FAIRBANKS** in the Delta Junction/ Big Delta area. In 1978, the state sold the agricultural rights to 65,000 acres of land to 22 farmers on relatively easy terms to encourage commercial barley production. High hopes that the area would prove to be Alaska's breadbasket have not borne fruit because of poor weather, poor crops, inexperience and an inadequate market.

DENA'INA (duh ny' nuh) — Alternate, and anthropologically preferred spelling of **TANAINA**, the name of the **ATHABASKAN** group that inhabit the coastal areas along **COOK INLET**.

DENALI (duh na' lee) — (1) Tanana **ATHABASKAN** word that means "the great one" or "the high one," referring to 20,320-foot high **MOUNT MCKINLEY**; (2) the 5.7-million acre national park in **INTERIOR** Alaska that surrounds Mount McKinley; (3) the 421,000-acre state park that abuts the national park; (4) gravel highway that connects the Richardson Highway with the **PARKS HIGHWAY** and Denali National Park.

"and we knew that, behind that damn cloud, stretched the majestic beauty of the 'highest peak on the North American Continent."

DENALI

DEVELOPER

DEVELOPER — Depending on who's talking, (a) the lifeblood of the American capitalist system, an enterprising hardworking person who is helping Alaska to reach its economic destiny, (b) a destructive individual dedicated to exploiting as many of Alaska's resources and turning them into as much cash as possible, (c) one who takes raw land and turns it into something else; most often used either as a compliment, a pejorative, or a boast.

DEVIL'S CLUB — Broad-leafed, sharp-spined plant that grows in Alaska's woodlands, where it is a hazard for the unwary hiker who grabs one for support or tries to brush one out of the way. Both the leaves and stems are spiny, the stems more so. It is a totally inhospitable plant that also produces inedible shiny red berries.

DEW (doo) LINE — Distant Early Warning Line, a system of radar scanning stations in **ARCTIC** Alaska and Canada, installed in the mid-1950s to detect incoming aircraft and provide a warning of potential attacks on either country; supplemented in 1961 by the Ballistic Missile Early Warning System, which was designed to detect incoming missiles.

DILLINGHAM (dil' ing ham) — Largest community near **BRISTOL BAY**, located at the junction of the Wood and Nushagak (nush' uh gak) rivers; named for William Paul Dillingham, U.S. Senator from Vermont, who toured Alaska with his subcommittee in 1903 and became the Senate's authority on the territory, along with Senator Knute Nelson of Minnesota, who was with him on the tour.

DIOMEDE (dy' uh meed) ISLANDS — Two islands in the **BERING** Strait separated by the border between the United States and the USSR and inhabited by members of the same **IN-UPIAT ESKIMO** families, who are kept apart by political tensions between the two countries. Little Diomede Island, on the U.S. side, is only three miles from the Soviet border. In the summer of 1987, Lynn Cox, an intrepid young long-distance swimmer, achieved a

HELLSPAWN FLORA
(DEVIL'S CLUB)

world record and international notoriety by becoming the first person to swim the frigid waters from one island to the other. In 1988, friendlier relations between the U.S. and the U.S.S.R. enabled island residents to visit their Russian relatives for the first time in more than 40 years.

DIP NETTING — Type of **SUBSISTENCE** fishing that allows one to stand at a river's edge and try to catch a **SALMON** in a conical net at the end of a long pole; a good excuse to get cold, tired and wet.

DOG BOX — Large rectangular box having several compartments, each with a hole at one end, carried on the bed of a truck or trailer to transport sled dogs to and from races and training sites.

DOG SALMON — Another name for **CHUM** salmon, Alaska's third most plentiful commercial species. There is disagreement about the origin of the name; some say it reflects **NATIVE** use of the fish to feed sled dog teams, others believe it comes from the fish's appearance when spawning, when its snout becomes hooked and teeth protrude from its mouth.

DOLLY VARDEN — Sea-run trout much prized as a sports fish in Alaska, both for the fight it puts up on the end of a line and for its succulent flesh, which tastes like a cross between **SALMON** and trout; named for its coloration after a type of dress and character in Charles Dickens' **Barnaby Rudge**; usually just called Dolly.

DOUGLAS — (1)Island and community that forms a suburb of **JUNEAU** and former site of one of the largest gold mining operations in Alaska, the Treadwell Mines; (2) cape and 7,064-foot mountain on the east side of the Alaska **PENINSULA** near the mouth of **COOK INLET**.

DREDGE (drej) — Machine used to haul dirt, rock and gravel from the bottom of a body of water and put it somewhere else; used in prospecting for gold and in enlarging harbors; as a verb, it refers to the process.

DRIFTER — (1)Drift gill net fisherman; (2) when preceded by the phrase "High Plains," a nickname for Gov. Steve Cowper (koo' pur), Alaska's seventh governor, elected in 1986.

DRILLING RIG — Equipment used to drill for oil either on land or offshore. Offshore rigs are affixed to **PLATFORMS**, several of which can be seen in upper **COOK INLET**.

D-2 LANDS — Lands set aside by Congress for parks and wildlife preserves under the Alaska National Interest Lands Conservation Act of 1980, as provided under subparagraph (d)(2) of Section 17 of the **ALASKA NATIVE CLAIMS SETTLEMENT ACT**. Under the provision, more than 100 million acres were included in land and wildlife conservation units throughout the state.

DUNGIE (dun' jee) — Dungeness crab, the smallest and, some say, tastiest of Alaska's three commercial species of crab; adults average two to three pounds; usually sold and served whole; named for a coastal fishing village in Washington.

DUTCH HARBOR — **ALEUTIAN ISLAND** fishing community and former military station bombed by the Japanese in World War II; named by the early Russian fur hunters, who thought the harbor was first visited by a Dutch vessel.

E

EAGLE — (1)Small Yukon River settlement six miles west of the U.S.-Canadian border, established in 1874 as a trading post for **KLONDIKE** gold miners; (2) large bird of prey, having a wing span of nearly seven feet, frequently seen in Alaskan skies. Alaska has two varieties of eagles: bald and golden. The golden, imperceptibly smaller than the bald, inhabits **INTERIOR** Alaska and alpine areas of the **KENAI PENINSULA** in the summer months. The bald, so-called because of its white head, is mainly a coastal dweller and can often be seen in communities such as **SITKA, JUNEAU, HAINES, KODIAK** and **HOMER**. The **CHILKAT** River valley, north of Haines, is said to have the continent's largest concentration of bald eagles in the winter, when hundreds dot the trees, but Homer and Cooper Landing in **SOUTHCENTRAL** Alaska and Kodiak also have fair-sized winter populations.

EAR PULL — Contest in the **WORLD ESKIMO INDIAN OLYMPICS**; a tug of war between two individuals, each tugging against a thin nylon string looped round the ear; the first person to give in to pain and let the string go slack or slip off the ear is the loser. It is a test of the individual's ability to withstand pain.

EAR WEIGHT — Another event in the **WORLD ESKIMO INDIAN OLYMPICS**; contestants see how far they can carry 16 pounds suspended from a piece of twine that is looped around one ear; the record is more than half a mile.

EGAN, WILLIAM A. — First Governor of Alaska elected after **STATEHOOD**; served from 1959-1966 and was re-elected for another four-year term in 1970. Known as Governor Bill, it is said he had the knack of remembering the name of nearly everyone he'd ever met.

EIELSON (y' uhl suhn) AIR FORCE BASE — U.S. air base near **FAIRBANKS**; at the time of its construction in 1943, said to have the largest runway in the world; usually called just Eielson; named for pioneer Alaska pilot Ben Eielson, who flew the first official Alaska air mail flight in 1924 and flew over the North Pole in 1928. He died in Siberia in 1929 while airlifting furs from an icebound schooner. A look-out point and visitor center in DENALI National Park also bears his name.

ELMENDORF (el' muhn dorf) **AIR FORCE BASE —** U.S. air base in **ANCHORAGE**; activated in 1940 as an adjunct to the Army's **FORT RICHARDSON**; usually called just Elmendorf; named for Captain Hugh Elmendorf, who was killed in an air crash at Wright Field, Ohio, in 1933.

ESKIMO (es' kuh mo) — One of Alaska's three major **NATIVE** groups, linguistically divided into the **INUPIAT** (in oo' pee at) or northern Eskimos, **YUPIK** (yoo' pik) or western Eskimos, and Sugpiaq (soog' pee ak) or Aleutiiq (al' eeoo tik), or Pacific, Eskimos (who generally consider themselves Aleuts); believed to have come to Alaska from Asia about 6,000 years ago; developers of the **PARKA, KAYAK** and harpoon. The Eskimos have taught us much about cold weather survival techniques and gear and have contributed much to the world's store of ethnic artwork. In Alaska, most still live a **SUBSISTENCE** lifestyle.

ESKIMO ICE CREAM — Confection popular with **NATIVES**, made from a mixture of berries, seal oil or other fat and snow whipped together, sometimes with sugar added; called akutak in **YUPIK**.

ESKIMO OLYMPICS — Short term for the **WORLD ESKIMO INDIAN OLYMPICS, NATIVE** games held each July in **FAIRBANKS**; features traditional games such as the **KNUCKLE HOP, BLANKET TOSS, STICK PULL, EAR PULL** and **TWO-FOOT HIGH KICK**. The games are tests of skill and endurance and those who perform them well are much honored.

EYAK (ee' ak) — An **ATHABASKAN**-speaking group that lived near **CORDOVA**, in the Copper River delta area on the Gulf of Alaska, now nearly completely assimilated into other **NATIVE** groups. The aboriginal culture was a mixture of Athabaskan, **TLINGIT** and Pacific **ESKIMO** traits.

F

FAIRBANKS — **GOLD RUSH** town in **INTERIOR** Alaska that survived to become Alaska's second largest city, the site of the first state university campus, the terminus of the **ALCAN** Highway, and the starting place for the Prudhoc Bay **HAUL ROAD**. It's a community people either love or hate, and a friendly rivalry exists between it and its large neighbor to the south, **AN-CHORAGE**. Established in 1903, it now has a population of over 75,000 and is known as the unofficial capital of the **INTERIOR**. As the nearest large community to **PRUDHOE BAY**, it boomed during construction of the **PIPELINE**. It was named at the suggestion of Judge James Wickersham for Indiana Senator James Fairbanks, who became vice president in the Theodore Roosevelt administration.

FIREWEED — One of Alaska's most spectacular flowers, consisting of a stalk of fuschia-colored blossoms, which grows in masses along hills, fields, and roadsides. It thrives where fires have burned back forested growth and is one of the first plants to appear after a burn; some say that accounts for its name, others say the name derives from the way it seems to blaze across hillsides in the late summer. It is just about the last plant to flower in the Alaska summer; when the blossoms die, the leaves turn bright red and the seeds sail outward on the wind, autumn has arrived. Oldtimers say when the fireweed is thick, it will be a heavy snow year.

FISH BURNER — Nickname for a dog, so called because rural **NATIVES** and other owners of sled dogs often feed their animals large quantities of dried fish.

FISH AND FEATHERS — Nickname for federal and state fish and wildlife management agencies; usually used pejoratively.

FISH AND GAME — What most Alaskans call the Alaska Dept. of Fish and Game, the agency responsible for managing the state's wildlife resources (except for sea mammals and migratory waterfowl, which are managed by the U.S. **FISH AND WILDLIFE** Service). Management generally means trying to make sure there are enough game animals for residents and visitors to hunt, and is accomplished by **PREDATOR CONTROL**, enhancing or protecting habitat, and regulating hunting. Hunting and fishing regulations are determined by boards, the members of which are appointed by the governor. Public input comes from local advisory boards and public hearings.

FISH AND WILDLIFE — U.S. Fish and Wildlife Service, the federal agency that manages **MARINE MAMMALS** in Alaskan waters and also manages the various wildlife **REFUGES** in the state. While **FISH AND GAME** manages the land mammals, Fish and Wildlife manages the land on these refuges and can open or close hunting or trapping on refuge lands. Some people say the federal agency tends to be more interested in the animals for their own sake rather than as game, while the reverse often appears to be true with the state agency.

FISH TRAP — Now outlawed device once used by canneries to catch millions of **SALMON** as they clustered at the mouth of spawning streams. It channeled fish into a penned area from which there was no escape. Its use was opposed by independent fishermen who felt not enough fish were being allowed to spawn to protect the fisheries and that they weren't getting their fair share of the catch. One of the first acts of the state Legislature after **STATEHOOD** was to officially outlaw use of the device in Alaskan waters.

FISH WHEEL — Wood and net SUBSISTENCE fishing contraption that uses the river current to move baskets that scoop fish out of the water; resembles a paddlewheel on an old-time river boat. The idea was introduced to the Indians of the Pacific west coast by the Spaniards and spread to Alaska before the first explorers arrived.

FLARING — The practice of igniting natural gas produced as a by-product of oil development. The flares look like giant candles and are so bright at times they show up on satellite pictures of the earth. The practice has provoked some controversy. Proponents say some flaring must be done to operate wells safely; opponents say companies flare because it's easier. Theoretically, the companies have no market for the gas and no economical way to get to market if they did have one; however, a natural gas pipeline from the NORTH SLOPE to the American midwest and east coast has been considered and may one day be built.

FLOAT — (1) buoyant device used to mark fishing nets or lines; (2) floating platform in a harbor used for mooring and landing; (3) gear attached to small planes to allow them to taxi and land on water.

FORAKER (for' uh ker) — Shortened version of MOUNT FORAKER.

FORGET-ME-NOT — Alaska's state flower; a small blue blossom, with five petals and a yellow and white center, which grows in clusters at the top of a single 9-12 inch stalk, and which somehow never fails to cheer; it is a frequent subject for Alaska pottery and jewelry decoration.

FORT GREELEY — U.S. Army base near Delta Junction that began existence in 1942 as the U.S. Army Air Corps' Big Delta airfield; in 1948, it became the Army's Arctic Test Center. When the base was enlarged in 1955, it was renamed in honor of Major

YOU'D BETTER HIT THE LIGHTS, DEAR. I KNOW IT'S EARLY, BUT IT'S GETTING PRETTY DARK.

FROST HEAVE

General Adolphus Washington Greeley, **ARCTIC** explorer and founder of the Alaska Communications System (see **ALASCOM**).

FORT RICHARDSON — U.S. Army base located in **AN-CHORAGE**; built in 1940 and named for General Wilds Preston Richardson, first president of the Alaska Road Commission and the man who laid out the trail between **VALDEZ** and **FAIRBANKS** that eventually became the Richardson Highway. Frequently called Fort Rich.

FORT WAINRIGHT — U.S. Army base near **FAIRBANKS**; activated as the Army Air Corps' Ladd Field in 1940; transferred to Army jurisdiction in 1961 and renamed for General Jonathan M. Wainright, World War II hero of Bataan. Not to be confused with Wainright, an **ESKIMO** village on the **ARCTIC** Ocean southwest of **BARROW**.

FOURTH AVENUE — Term that connotes Skid Row for **AN-CHORAGE** residents because of its two- or three-block section of bars and flophouses and because of the frequent presence of reeling drunks. Every large community in Alaska has an equivalent.

FREEZE-UP — The true beginning of winter in Alaska, usually sometime in October or November, when everything that can freeze, does; the opposite of **BREAK-UP**.

FROST HEAVE — A break or bump in the road caused by the swelling of frozen ground below the surface, especially noticeable during **BREAK-UP**. The swelling often disappears with the thaw, but may leave behind a road in much need of repair.

FRY — (1)Immature fish; (2) the only way some people cook fish.

FUR RONDY — Short name for the Anchorage Fur Rendezvous (ron' dee voo), an annual mid-winter celebration used as a curative for **CABIN FEVER**; includes games, parades, dances, contests, costumes, art and talent shows, and sled dog races. Called by some the Mardi Gras of the north, the week-long celebration began in 1936 as a fur market and over the years developed into the most exciting event of the year for many **SOUTHCENTRAL** Alaskans. Most popular events include the Miners and Trappers Costume Ball, the three-day, 75-mile World Championship Sled Dog Race, and the World Champion Dog Weight Pulling Contest.

G

GANGLINE — Main line running from dog sled to which dogs are attached by other lines; also called tow line.

GEE — Command to dog team to turn right. See also **HAW** and **MUSH**.

GIANT — High pressure hydraulic hose used to blast material out of a bank or hillside in **PLACER** gold mining.

GILL NETTER — Commercial fishing boat or operator that sets nets upright in the water to entangle salmon as they try to swim through; accounts for about half the approximately 100 million salmon commercially caught in Alaska each year. There are two types of gill netters; **DRIFTERS** and **SET NETTERS**. See also **SET**.

GLACIER (glay' shur) — (1) River or fall of ice composed of snow that has been compressed and built up over the centuries and is usually icy turquoise blue along its face, which moves forward as it grows and recedes as it either melts or **CALVES**. A galloping glacier is one that grows very fast, as much as 300 feet a day. In 1986, the Hubbard Glacier surged forward, damming a fjord and for a time trapping seals and other sea mammals behind a wall of ice. Glaciers cover about 300,000 square miles or 5 percent of Alaska. (2) As a verb, to cover a portion of road or path in winter with an uneven mass of ice, usually caused by a continual seepage of water over the roadway.

GLACIER BAY — National Monument established in 1925 in **SOUTHEAST** Alaska that contains over a dozen glaciers in its 3,600 square miles; summer feeding ground of the **HUMPBACK** whale; named in 1880 by U.S. Naval Captain L.A. Beardslee, but originally called "Big Ice Mountain Bay" by the **TLINGITS**.

GLARE ICE — Solid sheet of ice, often covered with a layer of water, that covers highways and parking lots in the **BANANA BELT**. See also **BLACK ICE**.

GOLD PAN — Wide, shallow metal pan resembling a large pie pan without the rim, used by prospectors to sample the gold potential of streams. The miners would scoop up a panful of water and streambed and slosh it around until the gold settled out. Pans are still used by prospectors, but are most often seen now in gift shops, sometimes decorated with handpainted Alaska scenes.

GOLD RUSH — The period between 1897 and 1901, when thousands of men and some women flocked to and through Alaska in search of gold, primarily headed toward the **KLONDIKE** or **NOME**; the first impetus for growth in American Alaska; the first sign that Alaska had more than furs to offer those who sought to tap its wealth. Other major gold finds in Alaska included **JUNEAU**, which accounted for nearly $150 million in gold from 1880-1944, and **FAIRBANKS**, which has been mined for gold off and on from 1903 to the present.

GOOD FRIDAY EARTHQUAKE — The state's largest and most devastating earthquake, which rocked **SOUTHCENTRAL** Alaska on March 27, 1964. Registering between 9.2 on the Richter scale, it tore up highways, tumbled houses into **TURNAGAIN ARM**, knocked downtown **ANCHORAGE** businesses off their foundations, caused an estimated $206 million in damages and left 2,000 homeless in Anchorage alone. Although its epicenter, or point of origin, was in **PRINCE WILLIAM SOUND**, it generated **TSUNAMIS** that ranged as far south as the northern coast of California and killed 131 people. In Alaska, tsunamis wiped out the town of **VALDEZ**, the harbor in **KODIAK**, and the waterfront in **SEWARD**, as well as many smaller communities.

GRAYLING — Small (under five pounds) but popular fresh water sports fish, found in cold water streams and lakes throughout **INTERIOR** Alaska and distinguished by its large dorsal fin.

GRAZING LEASE — Lease of state agricultural land specifically for livestock grazing or hay production, usually at extremely low rents. Some of these leases were originally granted by the **B.L.M.** for 55-year periods and were subsequently turned over to the state government, which manages them through the Dept. of Natural Resources, Division of Land and Water Management, and which retains all other rights to the use of the leased land. Tens of thousands of acres of Alaska land are covered by such leases.

GREAT LAND — What Alaskans sometimes like to call their state, partly because that's what Alaska's original name, **ALYESKA**, meant and partly because that's how they see it.

GRIZZLY — Another name for brown **BEAR**, referring specifically to one whose coat is tipped with light colored, blond or silver hairs, a color phase generally restricted to inland Alaska.

GRUBSTAKE — (1) The food, supplies and equipment, or the money to purchase them, provided by an outside party to a gold seeker in return for a share of the findings; (2) as a verb, to furnish supplies or money to a prospector.

GRUENING (gree' ning) ERNEST — Territorial governor of Alaska 1935-1953 and U.S. Senator from Alaska 1956-1968. He worked tirelessly for **STATEHOOD**, favored settlement of **NATIVE** land claims, and argued against the Vietnam War. He was defeated in his bid for re-election in 1968 by Mike Gravel (gruh vel'), who appealed to the voters as a younger man. The defeat was considered one of the great upsets of Alaskan politics.

GUILLOTINE (gil' uh teen) — Machine that cuts off the head of fish being processed in a **CANNERY**.

GULF COAST — The part of mainland Alaska that borders the Gulf of Alaska.

GUSSUK (guhs' uhk) — **ESKIMO** term for a caucasian, sometimes used disparagingly, said to originate from the Russian word "Cossack."

H

HAIDA (hy' duh) — One of Alaska's three **SOUTHEAST** Alaska Indian groups, believed to have moved north from the Queen Charlotte Islands of British Columbia in the 17th and 18th centuries. Renowned boat builders and **TOTEM** carvers, they shared many cultural characteristics with the other Southeast Alaska groups and with other Pacific Northwest Indians, including **CLAN** kinship, highly stylized artwork and rigidly stratified society.

GUILLOTINE.

HAINES (haynz) — Community of about 1,000 people in **SOUTHEAST** Alaska; end of the **INSIDE PASSAGE** for many tourists, who then drive across a corner of Canada into the rest of Alaska; originally a trading center for **CHILKAT TLINGITS** and **INTERIOR** Indians, who called it "Dtehsuh," meaning "end of the trail"; named by Presbyterian missionaries after a member of the board of missionaries.

HALIBUT (hal' uh but) — Large, white-fleshed, mild-tasting flat fish much sought by many commercial and charter fishing boats; so many boats go after halibut that the huge catch has resulted in limited commercial fishing seasons of one or two days two or three times a year; a fish that starts life with an eye on either side of the head but ends up with both on one side by the time it reaches maturity. The record caught was about 460 pounds. See **BARNDOOR** or **SOAKER**, also **CHICKEN**. Extremely small halibut are sometimes called ping pong paddles.

HARDHEAD — Affectionate term for commercial fishermen of Norwegian ancestry, used especially during the early part of this century when many Scandinavian fishermen came to Alaska.

HATCHERY — Fish hatchery, where **SALMON FRY** are raised. The immature fish are later released into bays, streams or rivers, to which they will return, after a sojourn in the Pacific Ocean, as mature **SPAWNING** salmon.

ʻIAUL ROAD — Formally the **NORTH SLOPE** Haul Road, now called the **DALTON HIGHWAY**, the 416-mile gravel highway from **FAIRBANKS** to **PRUDHOE BAY** used to haul freight and equipment to the oil fields.

HAW — Command to sled dog team to turn left. See also **GEE** and **MUSH**.

HICKEL (hik' uhl), WALTER J. — Second governor of Alaska following statehood, elected in 1966 and resigned in 1969 when he was appointed U.S. Secretary of Interior by then President Richard Nixon; returned to Alaska when he was forced to resign his post after making public a dispute with the president; subsequently ran for governor several times but was never able to retain the popularity he enjoyed in the mid-1960s; namesake of the **HICKEL HIGHWAY**.

HICKEL HIGHWAY — First road to the **NORTH SLOPE**, built to haul freight and equipment for the early oil development there. Hurriedly built, it was an economic and environmental disaster — because of melting **PERMAFROST**, it turned into a canal in the summer and could only be used in the winter, and freight cost as much to send that way as by plane.

HIGH BUSH CRANBERRY — A musty-smelling, sharp-tasting, transluscent red berry that resembles a large red currant but grows in smaller clusters; used by cooks for making a meat sauce, jelly, or homemade wine.

HIGHLINER — Term used for commercial fishermen who catch the largest quantities of fish in any given year.

HOMER — Small fishing and agricultural community of about 4,000 people on the northern shore of **KACHEMAK BAY** in **SOUTHCENTRAL** Alaska; named in 1896 for Homer Pennock, a member and promoter of a gold mining consortium, the Alaska Gold Mining Company. Now a tourist mecca because of its scenery and sports fishing opportunities, the area first drew people because of its coal reserves (still available for the gathering along local beaches during minus tides). The town also boasts one of the most active arts communities in the state.

HOMESTEAD — Land acquired from the government through **SWEAT EQUITY**, or hard work. Under the federal homestead program, which ended in Alaska with **STATEHOOD**, individuals could claim up to 160 acres by registering their claims, building a **PROVE-UP** cabin, clearing and planting a portion of the land, and living on the land for a given period of time. Meant to encourage agriculture, most of the state's original homesteads have wound up as subdivisions. The state government replaced homesteading with its own **LAND DISPOSAL** programs, most of which involve smaller parcels of land.

HOOK — (1) Barbed piece of metal attached to the end of a length of line, used for catching fish; (2) for commercial fishermen, a seine net laid out for fishing.

HOOK AND RELEASE — Practice of catching fish and then releasing them, followed by some sports fishermen who enjoy the fishing but not the killing and eating of their catch. Looked on with disdain by **SUBSISTENCE** and commercial fishermen.

HOPE — Tiny town of slightly more than 100 people on the south side of **TURNAGAIN ARM**; originally settled in 1896 as a gold mining town and called Hope City, for obvious reasons. At one time about 7,000 gold miners lived in the area.

HOOLIGAN (hoo' li guhn) — What Alaskans call eulachon, a small, narrow fish, much like a smelt, and much enjoyed by both humans and **BELUGA** whales; also called **CANDLEFISH** because it is so oily it can be burned. It is usually fished by **DIP NETTING**.

HUMMOCK (huhm' uhk) — Small area of land rising above the general level of a bog or marsh; area of matted grass and other growth that sticks up above surrounding growth and makes walking cross country very difficult. Also called a tussock.

HUMPBACK WHALE — **BALEEN** whale that summers in

A HOOLIGAN AT FRY SCHOOL.
(OR, WHEN FISH GO BAD....)

the waters of **GLACIER BAY** and that has become known as the singer of the seas.

HUMPY — Humpback or pink **SALMON**, the smallest of Alaska's five species of salmon, and one less prized by sports fishermen; caught by the tens of millions for commercial and **SUBSISTENCE** use, and generally canned. The nickname comes from the hump formed on the back of **SPAWNING** adult males. The record caught was 12 lb. 9 oz. and measured 30 inches.

HUNDRED-MILE-AN-HOUR-TAPE — Duct tape, used by pilots of small planes to fix tears in fabric covering and used by fishermen to temporarily fix just about everything; an indispensable ingredient in every Alaska tool kit.

HUSKY — Wolf-like dog very popular in Alaska and often used for sled dog races; resembles the **MALEMUTE** but is smaller and often has light eyes. It is not recognized by the American Kennel Club, which says the only true husky is a Siberian husky.

HYPOTHERMIA (hy po thur' mee uh) — Condition in which the body temperature is severely reduced, sometimes resulting in collapse or death, that affects people such as hikers and boaters who are inadequately garbed for long exposure to cold and wet.

I

ICE CREEPERS — Spiked plates that attach to soles of boots

HUNDRED-MILE AN HOUR TAPE.

or shoes by rubber straps and enable pedestrians to safely negotiate streets, sidewalks, and parking lots during **GLARE ICE** conditions; Alaska lifesavers.

ICE FIELD — Large area of permanent ice, found in mountainous areas and often connecting several glaciers. Ice fields in **SOUTHCENTRAL** Alaska include Harding Icefield, between **SEWARD** and the head of **KACHEMAK** Bay, Sargeant Icefield, between Seward and **PRINCE WILLIAM SOUND**, and the Bagley Icefield, in the **CHUGACH** Mountains between **CORDOVA** and **YAKUTAT**.

ICE FOG — Winter condition in which the air is full of a zillion crystals of ice, leaving fences, trees and anything else that isn't moving outlined in rime; occurs at subzero temperatures in communities along ocean and river fronts, but especially noticable in **FAIRBANKS**, where a combination of temperature inversions and auto and chimney emissions produce ice fog so thick it rivals London at its worst.

ICEWORM — Small worm living in glaciers and occasionally seen on dim, overcast days or during the hours of dawn and dusk. Frequently, and mistakenly, thought to be merely a figment of some fertile imagination created to confuse **CHEECHAKOS**, they were actually discovered in 1887. They measure about an inch in length, may be yellow, white, brown or black, and survive on airborne pollen grains, fern spores and algae that grows in the snow.

IDITAROD (y dit' uh rod) — As in "the" Iditarod, the annual 1,000-plus mile sled dog race from **ANCHORAGE** to **NOME** that challenges the stamina and determination of men and women and their dogs. It commemorates the 1925 emergency run to bring diphtheria vaccine to Nome to head off an anticipated epidemic; 20 dog teams relayed 300,000 units of serum 674 miles, from **NENANA** to Nome, in 127½ hours, or a little over five days. The modern race is not a relay, and the fastest run that has been made is 11½ days, run by Susan Butcher in 1987. Follows the dog team

INUPIAT, INUPIAQ (in oo' pee at) — Northern or ARCTIC Alaska **ESKIMOS**, whose territory extends as far south on the **BERING** Sea as Norton **SOUND**. Coastal dwellers were, and some still are, primarily sea mammal hunters, relying on **BOWHEAD** whales, walrus and seals for **SUBSISTENCE**; those in the INTERIOR rely primarily on the **CARIBOU**. See also **YUPIK**.

IRISH LORD — An incredibly ugly, spiny fish that turns up on the end of a line with irritating frequency when one is fishing coastal waters for **SALMON** or **HALIBUT**; a type of sculpin.

J

JACKS — Young king **SALMON** that are not fully grown.

JACKSON, SHELDON — Presbyterian educator who served as General Agent for Education in Alaska from 1884-1908, who solved the problem of having too little money to build schools by encouraging various Protestant churches to establish missions and schools throughout the territory, and who sought to solve the problem of hunger in Northwestern Alaska by importing **REINDEER** to be raised as a domestic replacement for **CARIBOU** and other **SUBSISTENCE** species. A college and a museum in **SITKA** bear his name.

JIG — (1) Noun, a fishing lure; (2) verb, to bob one's lure up and down in hopes of attracting a fish; (3) noun, what one feels like dancing after landing a big one.

SOUTHEAST Alaska, east of SITKA and southwest of JUNEAU.

KASHIM (ka sheem') — ESKIMO meeting and ceremonial house.

KATMAI (kat' my) — (1) One of Alaska's 35 active volcanoes, a 6,970-foot-high peak on the Alaska Peninsula that erupted in June 1912 and sent ash tens of thousands of feet into the air, coloring sunsets around the world for years and burying KODIAK under 18 inches of grit; (2) National Park that encompasses Mount Katmai and the Valley of 10,000 Smokes, so named because of the many fumaroles explorers saw soon after the eruption.

KAYAK (ky' ak) — Traditionally, a narrow skin boat pointed at both ends, covered top and bottom, having a hole in the top center for the boat operator, and propelled by a single oar with paddles on both ends, developed and used by the ESKIMOS for hunting sea mammals; now, a boat made from any material along the same design; the Eskimo version of the ALEUT BIDARKA.

KENAI (kee' ny) — (1)PENINSULA in SOUTHCENTRAL Alaska bordered by COOK Inlet and the Gulf of Alaska; (2) city of about 6,500 people on that peninsula that, with its sister city of SOLDOTNA, is both the center of population on the peninsula and the center of oil development in the area; (3) river in the same area known primarily for its sports fishing opportunities; (4) lake located between Cooper Landing and SEWARD, south of ANCHORAGE, known primarily as a summer resort area. The name derives from the Kenaitze (kee ny' tsee) Tribe of the DENA'INA Indians. Kenaitze is a Russianized version of the Chugach Eskimo word for the Dena'ina who called the peninsula "Yaghanen," or the good land.

KETCHIKAN (kech' uh kan) — Community of about 14,000 people on Revillagigedo (ruh vee uh guh gay' do, now usually shortened to ruh vil' uh) Island in **SOUTHEAST** Alaska; built as a fishing town around a cannery in 1887, became a gold field supply town in the 1890s, and now relies on fishing and timber; first Alaskan port of call for cruise ships sailing the **INSIDE PASSAGE**. The name is an Anglified version of the **TLINGIT** name "Ketschkhin," which folklore says means "eagle wing river" and refers to the pattern a nearby waterfall makes breaking around a boulder.

KICKER — (1)**BUSH** term for an outboard motor; the bowed portion of a **NORDIC SKI** that lies directly beneath the sole plate.

KING CRAB — The biggest and most famous crab in Alaskan waters, the crab most often seen on trophy walls and requested by visiting diners. It is not a true crab, having only eight legs instead of 10, but that doesn't detract from its popularity or its taste. Commercially caught males average about seven pounds and measure about a yard across with legs outstretched, but they have been known to weigh almost 25 pounds. While it is arguably the most publicly popular of Alaska's shellfish, it is not the most abundant. Of more than 148 million pounds of shellfish harvested commercially in 1986, 110 million pounds were **TANNER** crab and only 27 million king crab.

KINGS — King salmon, Alaska's largest and one of its most popular **SALMON**, subject of several fishing derbies statewide; typically exceeds 30 pounds and has gone as high as 126 pounds; also called **CHINOOK**.

KISKA (kis' kuh) — One of three **ALEUTIAN ISLANDS** occupied by the Japanese during World War II and re-occupied by U.S. and Canadian forces in August of 1943. The battle to recapture the island was a true boondoggle: the Japanese had already left and the Allied forces ended up shooting at each other in the fog. Nearly 100 people were killed in the invasion, which involved close to 100 ships and 144,000 troops and cost $150 million to $170 million. See also **ATTU**.

KLISTER (klis' ter) — Gooey, sticky substance spread on waxable **NORDIC SKIS** to give them both traction and glide on snow that has melted and then refrozen; acts like glue for all other types of snow. It is the softest of the waxes used for skiing and must be scraped completely off before applying any other wax — usually at the beginning of winter, after a summer's worth of dust has stuck onto last spring's klister.

KLONDIKE — Site of the 1896 gold discovery that launched the 1897 **GOLD RUSH** and brought thousands of men and women to Alaska and Canada's **YUKON** Territory; the area surrounding the confluence of the Yukon and Klondike rivers, centering on **DAWSON** City.

KNIK (kuh nik') — Northernmost arm of **COOK INLET**; the major waterway between **ANCHORAGE** and the **MATANUSKA** Valley; small community that gains a little attention each year as a checkpoint on the **IDITAROD** Sled Dog Race.

KNUCKLE HOP — Grueling event in the **ESKIMO OLYMPICS** in which contestants lay on their stomachs and propel themselves across the floor by hopping on their knuckles, emulating the movements of seals on land. The winner is the one who hops the farthest. The record is 169 feet.

KODIAK (ko' dee ak) — Island and community in the Gulf of Alaska near the mouth of **COOK** Inlet. The island was the site of the first settlement in **RUSSIAN AMERICA**, at Three Saints Bay near the southern end of the island, became the site of cattle grazing operations in the 1950s, and gives its name to a large variety of brown **BEAR**. The community was the first capital of Alaska during the Russian American period and has gone on to become the state's number one fishing port. It serves about 2,000 vessels a year, which harvest **SALMON**, shrimp, **HALIBUT**, herring, white fish, and crab. The town was buried in 18 inches of ash after the **KATMAI** eruption of 1912, and was partially destroyed by a **TSUNAMI** following the **GOOD FRIDAY EARTHQUAKE** of 1964.

The community has a population of nearly 7,000 and can be reached only by plane or boat.

KOLOSH (kuh losh') — Russian name for the **TLINGIT** Indians, sometimes used pejoratively; a shortened version of the Russian term "kolushki," which meant "little platters" and referred to the wooden **LABRET**s worn by high caste Tlingit women.

KONIAG (ko' nee ag) — **ESKIMO**-speaking people who inhabited **KODIAK** Island when the Russians arrived.

KOTZEBUE (kot' zuh byoo) — **SOUND** and coastal **ESKIMO** village of about 2,000 people in Northwestern Alaska just north of the **ARCTIC** Circle; named for Russian explorer Otto von Kotzebue. The village is located on a three-mile long **SPIT**.

KUSKOKWIM (kus' ko kwim) — One of Alaska's major rivers, which runs from about the center of the state 540 miles southwest and empties into Kuskokwim Bay, on the **BERING** Sea north of **BRISTOL BAY**; mountain range that runs nearly the length of the river.

KUSPUK (kus puk') — **ESKIMO** woman's summer **PARKA**, made of cloth and decorated with fabric trim and sometimes fur, worn as a coat over outer clothing.

KVICHAK (kwee' jak) — River that runs from Lake **ILIAMNA** to **BRISTOL BAY** in Southwestern Alaska, at the upper end of the Alaska Peninsula, that is the target of millions of returning **SOCKEYE SALMON** each year.

L

LABRET (la' bret or luh bret') — Carved wood, ivory or bone ornament placed through an incision in the cheek or lip of aboriginal **ESKIMOS, TLINGITS**, and some **ATHABASKANS**, and worn as jewelry; a prehistoric equivalent of pierced ears that no longer occurs.

LAND DISPOSAL — Conveyance of state-owned land to private holders by sale. Purchasers used to stake out a claim of up to five acres on **OPEN-TO-ENTRY LAND**, apply for purchase, and after meeting certain state requirements could buy the land at the assessed value of nearby land. Agricultural leaseholders also sometimes bought part of their holdings from the state. Then the state switched to auctioning off selected parcels of its land, but that inflated land values and gave **DEVELOPERS** an edge over the average citizen. Now the purchaser is decided by chance. The Alaska Division of Land and Water Management decides what and how much land to convey, lets people bid on certain tracts, and then selects the winner by lottery. The land ranges from homesites to agricultural sites and from a few acres to over 100 acres. The price charged is assessed value of nearby land.

LAND LOTTERY — Process of choosing purchasers of state-owned land. Would-be buyers file an application for one, or more than one, of the parcels the state is offering and then wait for the lottery to find out if they've won; sometimes there's only one bidder on a parcel, sometimes several; winners pay the assessed value of similar land in the area.

LAND SWAP — Process of trading state-owned land for **NATIVE**-owned land for mutual benefit. Some land the state government wanted and had tentatively selected from federally-owned lands under the statehood act was selected by Native **REGIONAL CORPORATIONS** under the **ALASKA NATIVE CLAIMS SETTLEMENT ACT**; to get it back, the state is forced to try to swap land with the Natives, giving them in return land they can develop or turn to a profit elsewhere.

LANDING STRIP — Relatively small, flat — usually graded — area used for landing small aircraft.

LEAD DOG — Dog that runs at the front of a dog sled team, that knows the commands and keeps the team headed in the right direction; also called the leader.

LIMITED ENTRY — Legislative attempt to regulate the commercial harvest of **SALMON** by restricting it to those who hold permits and by assigning permits to specific areas. Original permits went to people who met eligibility requirements. Newcomers enter the industry by purchasing a permit from someone who has one. Permits, because they are limited, are worth thousands of dollars of income to their holders, either by catch or by sale.

LINE — (1) the length of material that goes from a fishing rod to the hook and that varies in thickness according to the size of the fish sought; (2) shortened version of trap line, a circuit followed by those who trap animals for sport or economic gain; (3) nickname for the redlight district in **GOLD RUSH** towns, the row of houses used by the town's prostitutes; (4) patter designed to attract members of the opposite sex.

LIVENGOOD (ly' vuhn gud) — Tiny community 50 miles northwest of **FAIRBANKS**, named for Jay Livengood, who discovered gold there in 1914.

LODE — Vein or deposit of metallic ore, primarily gold in Alaska; the "mother lode" is a large deposit, the quest of prospectors and miners everywhere.

LONGEVITY BONUS — Monthly stipend originally paid to Alaskan residents over the age of 65 years who had resided in the

LANDING STRIPE

state continuously for 25 years and subsequently paid to all Alaska senior citizens regardless of their length of residency, because of a successful constitutional challenge. The Alaska Legislature periodically tries to find a way to reward its pioneers without depriving other citizens of their rights and, at the same time, decrease the drain on public coffers. In 1988, it voted to turn the bonus into an annuity limited to seniors who contributed their **PERMANENT FUND** dividend checks to it, but the measure was vetoed by Gov. Steve Cowper (coo' per).

LONGLINER — Commercial **HALIBUT** and cod fishing operation that uses hooks and lines, rather than nets, to capture fish. The name comes from the practice of stringing sets of lines, called **SKATES**, together to form lines hundreds of feet long.

LOW BUSH CRANBERRY — Lingonberry, a small, deep red berry that resembles a miniature cranberry and grows in delightful profusion on low lying plants in forested areas; good for jams, jellies, pies and other desserts, wines and liqueurs.

LOWER 48 — What Alaskans call the 48 contiguous states that, with Hawaii, make up the rest of the United States. See also **OUTSIDE**.

M

MALASPINA (mal us spee' nuh) — **GLACIER** on the Gulf of Alaska near **YAKUTAT**; named for an Italian navigator and explorer who sailed for Spain and explored the northwest coast of America in 1791.

MALEMUTE, MALAMUTE (mal' uh myoot) — Large wolf-like dog that ranges in size from 50-115 pounds; one of Alaska's earliest sled dogs; characterized by a distinctive cap and mask; namesake of the Malemute Saloon, immortalized by poet Robert Service in "The Shooting of Dan McGrew." Originally used for freighting, it is larger than the HUSKY, which it resembles and with which it is sometimes confused. Another distinction is eye color: huskies sometimes have light eyes, but malemutes never do.

MARINE HIGHWAY — Alaska's ferry system. It connects coastal communities to the rest of Alaska, and is particularly important to island communities such as KODIAK and SITKA and the isolated communities along SOUTHEAST Alaska's INSIDE PASSAGE. There are three basic routes in the system, the Inside Passage, PRINCE WILLIAM SOUND, and the SOUTHCENTRAL GULF COAST; the routes do not cross and ferries which ply one route do not travel another. Major communities served by the Southeast route include JUNEAU, KETCHIKAN, PETERSBURG, HAINES and SKAGWAY; Prince William Sound communities are WHITTIER, VALDEZ and CORDOVA; the Gulf route includes HOMER, SELDOVIA, SEWARD, KODIAK and Sand Point, in the Shumagin Islands off the Alaska Peninsula.

MARINE MAMMAL — Any seagoing mammal, including whales, porpoises, seals, sea lions, walrus, sea otters and polar BEARS. Alaska's marine mammals are managed by the U.S. FISH AND WILDLIFE Service and are protected from hunting by anyone who is not a NATIVE. The state government has, from time to time, sought control of the animals in Alaska's coastal waters, and most recently is pursuing the idea of joint management. Whale hunting is further restricted by the International Whaling Commission, which has set quotas for Native SUBSISTENCE hunting of the BOWHEAD whale.

MATANUSKA (mat uh noo' skuh) — (1) Wide valley north of ANCHORAGE, best known for its farm products, which account for more than half of the state's agricultural output, and as

MARINE HIGHWAY

MOOSE — The largest of the deer family, weighing 800-1,600 pounds full grown; found throughout Alaska except for the **ALEUTIAN ISLANDS** and the islands of **SOUTHEAST** Alaska. Generally solitary animals except during the mating season and sometimes in winter. Males are called **BULLS** and females are called **COWS**. Only the males grow antlers, called a rack, which are wider, and more palmate than other deer antlers and have been known to grow to spans of nearly six and a half feet. This and their great size make them one of Alaska's most popular game and trophy animals. Cows give birth in the spring to single or twin calves (triplets are rare) that weigh about 30 pounds at birth and are bright rust color. **BEARS** and sometimes wolves are the primary predators for calves but pose little threat to mature, healthy adults. Moose are ruminants and spend most of their time wandering around snacking on fireweed shoots, grass, water plants, willow, birch and aspen leaves and, in winter, twigs, although they frequently display an overwhelming fondness for succulent garden produce and domestic fruit trees. They adapt fairly well to people and are often seen alongside roads, in towns and people's yards. They are a particular hazard for drivers at night or on icy roads because they are undeterred by traffic and step out onto the road whenever they feel like it.

MOOSE GOOSER — Alaska equivalent of the "cow catcher" on railroad engines in the **LOWER** 48; slang term for the Alaska Railroad, probably founded in the many right-of-way altercations between moose (which inevitably lose the battle) and the train.

MOSQUITO (muh skee' to) — The only drawback to summer in Alaska; the bane of hikers and campers and anyone else who wants to spend more than about 30 seconds outdoors in rural or **BUSH** Alaska; an irritating winged creature with a menacing whine and the nasty habit of not only taking one's blood but leaving behind an itchy memento of its visit. Where they are particularly thick they have been said to drive even wildlife wild; popular folklore contends that, in these areas, mosquitos can drain an incapacitated human dry in half an hour, and anyone who has heard them hitting the tent roof like miniature kamikaze pilots or tiny pellets of hail can readily believe it. Only the females

MOSQUITO

suck blood; males are guiltless vegetarians.

MOUNT AUGUSTINE — 4,000-foot-high volcano and island in **COOK INLET** in **SOUTHCENTRAL** Alaska that drew national attention when it erupted in 1976 and again in 1986. Dust from the 1976 eruption was carried by high altitude winds as far east as Nova Scotia, on Canada's east coast, and as far south as Tucson, Arizona. Named by Captain James Cook, who sighted it on St. Augustine's Day in 1778.

MOUNT FORAKER (for' uh ker) — 17,395-foot-high sister peak to Mount **McKINLEY**. The two are so closely connected, the Russians and some **TANAINA** Indians called them both by one name, but the **NATIVES** to the northwest of the mountains distinguished between the two and called Foraker "Sultana," meaning "the woman," or "Manhale," meaning "Denali's wife."

MOUNT MARATHON — 3,022-foot-high mountain that overlooks **SEWARD** in **SOUTHCENTRAL** Alaska; site of an annual Fourth of July race, said to have been started by two **SOURDOUGHS** who had a bet about how long it would take to run up the mountain and back. The fastest time so far is 43 minutes and 23 seconds. Experts say the longest part of the race is the uphill climb and that the downhill slide can be made in 10 minutes. The race draws hundreds of participants and observers each year.

MUD BOOTS — High-topped rubber boots worn by residents of rural areas during **BREAK-UP** and long periods of rainy weather, or on the beach gathering clams, mussels and other marine edibles; also called **BREAK-UP** boots, **CANNERY** boots, red-rubbers, and **SOUTHEAST** sneakers.

MUDFLATS — Coastal areas left high and not so dry by extreme tidal ebbs; a hazard to the unwary who wander out on them to search for clams and other marine bounty and sometimes become stuck in the thick, gelatinous ooze; also called tidal flats.

MUKLUK (muk' luk) — Ankle- or calf-high moccasins or boots traditionally made by **NATIVES** from seal skin, **CARIBOU**, or **MOOSE** and decorated with fur and beadwork; noted for being both lightweight and warm. There are two types: one with a hard **OOGRUK** sole that is good for snow, and one with a soft sole and fur on the inside that is good for cold weather and icy surfaces; traditionally insulated with replaceable dry moss or grass.

MUKLUK TELEGRAPH — Early name for sytem of sending messages over commercial radio to people who lived in the **BUSH** or who did not have telephones; refers specifically to **ANCHORAGE**, but other communities have their own equivalents, such as Northwinds or Bush Lines; illegal in other parts of the U.S., but approved in Alaska, where such messages are a boon and pick-me-up, and sometimes a necessity, for isolated rural Alaskans.

MUKTUK (muk' tuk) — Whale skin and **BLUBBER**, savored as a delicacy by **ESKIMOS** and eaten fresh or frozen, cooked or pickled; said to taste a little like coconut, a little like salt pork.

MURRES (merz) — Alaska's answer to the penguin; medium-sized black and white birds, marked much like penguins, that nest on rocky rookeries, lay their eggs on open ledges, and spend their winter months on the open sea. Penguins are not found in Alaska.

MUSH — (1) Command to get sled dogs moving (see also **GEE** and **HAW**); (2) to run a dog team and sled; (3) breakfast dish of boiled cereal or cornmeal, usually eaten as a last resort when nothing else is available.

MUSHER — A person who runs a dog sled team. Not to be confused with a masher, who is generally more interested in women than in dogs.

MUSKEG (mus' keg) — Humpy little bogs that cover much of Alaska; characterized by moss, acid soil and scraggly, spindly little black spruce, although the periphery may be lined with low-lying bog bilberry, or blueberry, and crowberry plants; another good place to wear **MUD BOOTS.**

MUSK OX — Stocky, long-haired, horned creature that looks like a cross between a water buffalo and a wooly mammoth and is rarely seen in the wild. Its underhair, shed each summer, is used for a yarn called **QIVIUT,** that is unbelievably light, soft and warm. Hunted to extinction in Alaska by the mid-1800s, the animal was reintroduced from Greenland and was ultimately transplanted to Nunivak (noo' nuh vak) Island and several other isolated areas along Alaska's northwest coast. The University of Alaska also maintains an experimental musk ox farm program.

N

NATIONAL PETROLEUM RESERVE — Proper name of **PET FOUR.**

NATIVE — One of Alaska's indigenous people, either **ESKIMO,** Indian (**ATHABASKAN, TLINGIT, HAIDA** and **TSIMPSHIAN**) or **ALEUT;** not to be confused with native, with a small "n," which is anyone born in the state, although most non-Native Alaskans born here just call themselves lifelong Alaskans.

NATIVE CORPORATION — Corporation set up under the **ALASKA NATIVE CLAIMS SETTLEMENT ACT** to provide con-tinuing income and economic stability for Alaska's **NATIVES,** by investing the money awarded under the act in various business endeavors.

ORCA (KILLER WHALE)

both beautiful and intelligent, they are also the darlings of several marine exhibits in the **LOWER** 48, where they have been trained to do a variety of tricks.

OUTSIDE — What Alaskans call every place but Alaska, with specific reference to the **LOWER** 48, or continental United States. Hundreds of Alaskans go Outside every winter, to warm and sunny locales where they don't have to worry about coats or boots or getting their noses frozen. So many go to Hawaii over the Christmas holidays that tickets have to be booked a year in advance, and Honolulu is said to become Alaska's second largest city.

P

PACK ICE — Large sheets of sea ice, from several feet to 15 feet in thickness, that form and drift in the **ARCTIC** Ocean; called in the aggregate the ice pack, and characterized by ridges and blocks of ice that are pushed up as the pack shifts, either against itself or against the shore. This movement causes some **CONSERVATIONISTS** and **NATIVES** to question the advisability of allowing offshore oil exploration and development in the Arctic Ocean. Unlike the Antarctic ice pack, the Arctic ice pack is not a solid, permanent feature of the landscape; in fall, winter and spring it extends from the shore north toward the pole, but in summer it recedes from the coastline, melts and breaks into small floating packs.

PAD — (1) Short for drilling pad, a flattened and smoothed, sometimes graveled, area that supports a **DRILLING RIG** and other equipment for tapping oil and gas reserves. In some areas, the only sign of past oil and gas exploration and development is an empty pad, looking rather like the parking lot of a defunct shopping mall. (2) A landing place for a helicopter.

PALMER — City of about 2,700 people in the **MATANUSKA** Valley that was established in 1916 by the Alaska Railroad, became the center of the **MATANUSKA VALLEY COLONY** experiment and **BOROUGH** government for the valley; site of **SOUTHCENTRAL**'s largest state fair, held every fall.

PANCAKE ICE — Sea ice that forms into small, flat, thin cakes that drift with the current and tide in winter or periods of very cold weather.

PANHANDLE — Slang for **SOUTHEAST** Alaska, that narrow fringe of land and islands between the Pacific Ocean and Canada, so called because it forms the handle to the pan formed by the rest of the state.

PARKA (par' kuh or par' kee) — Long, hooded jacket developed by the **ESKIMOS** and designed to keep the cold out and the warmth in; originally made of **CARIBOU** skin with fur trim, now made of a variety of furs and cloth and sometimes stuffed with down or other insulating material; traditionally sewn together with sinew, thread made from the long leg muscle or back tendon of a caribou, now usually sewn with dental floss. Women's parkas sometimes included a bulky recess at the inside back for carrying small children. In the wintertime, Eskimos sometimes wore two parkas, one with the fur facing the skin and the other with the fur facing outward. Fur parkas are considered fancy parkas today, and grandmothers delight in making them for their grandchildren.

PARKA SQUIRREL — Pronounced par' kee by oldtimers; common name for the **ARCTIC** ground squirrel, a plump, furry creature that gets up to about 18-inches long and resembles a prairie dog; found throughout Alaska, in open **TUNDRA** and on alpine hillsides. It adapts well to people and is a frequent visitor at camp or picnic sites in these areas, where it puts on a show of stuffing all it can into its cheek pouches. Its skin is sometimes used for **ESKIMO PARKAS**, which may account for its name.

PARKS HIGHWAY — Main highway north from **ANCHORAGE** to **FAIRBANKS**. Although it is also the most direct access from **SOUTHCENTRAL** to **DENALI** State Park and **McKINLEY** National Park, the 358-mile-long highway is not named for those parks but for George A. Parks, territorial governor of Alaska from 1925-1933.

PASS — Gap or opening in a mountain range that serves as a route of travel. See **CHILKAT** and **CHILKOOT PASS**.

PENINSULA — Thumb of land surrounded on three sides by water. Alaska's main peninsulas are the **KENAI** Peninsula in **SOUTHCENTRAL**, which is bordered by **COOK INLET** and the Gulf of Alaska; the Alaska Peninsula, which runs from Southcentral to Southwestern Alaska and is bound on one side by the Pacific Ocean and on the other by **BRISTOL BAY**; and the **SEWARD** Peninsula, in Northwest Alaska, which is bordered by Norton and **KOTZEBUE** Sounds and the **BERING** Sea.

PERMAFROST (per' muh frost) — Ground that stays perpetually frozen and prevents surface water from percolating through the soil, creating thousands of lakes and marshes throughout the summer; occurs where the mean average temperature is below 28 degrees Fahrenheit; most common in **INTERIOR** and **ARCTIC** areas, where the frost may go as deep as 2,000 feet, but also found as far south as **SOUTHCENTRAL** Alaska. Concern about possible environmental damage due to the melting of permafrost around buried pipe through which hot oil would be passing caused engineers to rethink their plans, thereby delaying the building of the **TRANS-ALASKA PIPELINE**. Some of the pipeline was buried, but surrounded by gravel to insulate it

PERMAFROST CONSTRUCTION TECHNIQUES.

and keep it from melting the permafrost; the rest was built above ground.

PERMANENT FUND — Alaska's rainy day money; a trust fund created by an amendment to the state constitution that sets aside a percentage of state oil and gas revenue for investment and protects it from government spending. Since 1982, Alaska residents have received an annual dividend of fund earnings, beginning with a $1,000 payment to every eligible man, woman and child in the state. For nearly the same amount of time, legislators have tried to figure a way to get at the funds, or at least at the earnings, without losing votes in the process.

PEROK (per ok') — Also called "piroshki" (per osh' kee) and "perogue" (per o' gee); a fish pie or turnover made with rice, vegetables, and **SALMON** and **HALIBUT**; said by some to be the best known dish among older Alaskans and **NATIVES**.

PERSONAL USE — A fishing category that allows non-**NATIVES** to use **SUBSISTENCE** methods to catch large numbers of **SALMON** for personal consumption. It is open to all Alaska residents, regardless of race, economic status, or location of residence. Personal use fish are usually taken with **SET NETS** laid along the beach at low tide and then cleaned at the next low tide.

PETERSBURG — Town of about 3,000 people on Mitkof Island in **SOUTHEAST** Alaska north of **WRANGELL**; grew up around a **SALMON CANNERY** and sawmill established in the late 1890s by Peter Buschmann, for whom it was named; also called "Little Norway" because of the many Scandinavians who settled there and patterned their homes and gardens after the ones they'd left behind in Northern Europe.

PET FOUR — Common name for U.S. Naval Petroleum Reserve No. 4, now National Petroleum Reserve, a 37,000-square-mile reserve in northwest Alaska, along the **ARCTIC** Slope from Icy Cape to the mouth of the Colville River. It was set aside in 1923 and explored and tested off and on until 1953, but was never developed. However, in 1981, the U.S. Dept. of Interior began a leasing program to encourage exploration and development, leasing more than 1.5 million acres.

PINKS — Plural reference to pink or humpback **SALMON**, smallest but most plentiful of Alaska's salmon, accounting for about half the annual commercial salmon catch or about 60 million fish; usually canned. See **HUMPY**.

PIONEER — Anyone who came to Alaska before 1960 and helped settle its communities; for residency in one of Alaska's Pioneer Homes, a pioneer is anyone 65 or older who has lived in the state continuously for 15 years; for membership in Pioneers of Alaska, a pioneer is a white male who has lived in Alaska at least 30 years.

PIPELINE — As in "the" pipeline, the $8 billion, 800-mile pipeline that transects the state and carries **NORTH SLOPE** oil from **PRUDHOE BAY** to **VALDEZ** for shipment in tankers to various U.S. ports. It was the source of a great deal of controversy in the early 1970s, pitting those who feared the pipeline would lead to the loss of wildlife and wilderness against those who thought the benefits of development outweighed the environmental risks. After four years of public comment and environmental study, in 1974 Congress overrode all objections and approved construction. The line was completed in 1977, but the controversy it provoked was never resolved and there is still disagreement about its ultimate impact.

PLACER (pla' ser) MINING — Surface mining for gold, primarily in river and streambeds; utilizes **GOLD PANS**, **ROCKERS** or **SLUICE BOXES** if the find is big enough, and sometimes high-power hydraulic hoses to break down the frozen ground. The bulk of Alaska gold mining was, and is, placer mining.

PLATFORM — Short for oil platform or drilling platform, a large structure that houses a **DRILLING RIG** and crew for offshore oil exploration and development. Upper **COOK INLET** is dotted by oil platforms. The offshore equivalent of a **PAD**.

PLUG-IN — Electrical outlet for a car engine heater, necessary on days of minus-30 degrees Fahrenheit and colder in order to keep car engines warm enough to start. In **FAIRBANKS**, where winter temperatures may drop as low as 60 degrees below zero on occasion, plug-ins are attached to some parking meters. Where plug-ins aren't offered, drivers sometimes leave their cars running during brief stops, so the engine won't freeze.

PORTAGE (por' tij, originally por tahzh') — (1) Noun, **GLACIER** and wayside in **SOUTHCENTRAL** Alaska, south of **ANCHORAGE**; (2) town destroyed in the **GOOD FRIDAY EARTHQUAKE** formerly located on **TURNAGAIN** Arm; (3) portion of a water transportation route that must be walked because of rough water or other interruption; (4) as a verb, to carry equipment and supplies overland between points on a water transportation route.

POT — Metal and twine contraption used for catching shrimp and crab.

POTLATCH (pot' lach) — **NATIVE** ceremony in which friends, relatives and neighbors gather for feasting, storytelling and dancing, and are given gifts by the potlatch host. In **TLINGIT** culture, potlatches were a way of gaining prestige and obligating others, the object being to give away more than any other potlatch host, thereby showing how wealthy one was. They grew so extravagant and expensive the federal government placed restrictions on them at the turn of the century. In **ATHABASKAN** culture, potlatches are usually held to commemorate a particular event, such as birth or death, and solidify community ties. Whatever the reason behind a potlatch, the effect was the distribution of wealth.

POWDER — Dry, lightweight snow that is the delight of skiers, especially when there are just a few inches on top of compacted snow, because it is easily moved through and doesn't stick to skis.

PREDATOR CONTROL — Removal of predatory species, like wolves or **BEARS**, from particular areas in hope that **MOOSE, CARIBOU,** or migratory bird populations will increase; usually involves the death of the predator through hunting, trapping, or baiting. When it's aimed at wolves it never fails to stir up a flurry of opposition from those who equate the animals with wilderness.

PRESERVATIONIST — Depending on who's talking, (1) a person who seeks to preserve and protect as much of the natural world as possible from despoilers and **DEVELOPERS** so that something remains untouched for future generations, or (2) a person who is anti-progress, anti-growth, anti-American, who values scenery and animals more than people, sometimes also called a posy-sniffer. See also **CONSERVATIONIST**

PRIBILOFS (prib uh lofs') — Two **BERING** Sea islands, St. Paul and St. George, also known as the Seal Islands for their crowded seal rookeries, which account for about 80 percent of the world's northern fur seal population. Millons of seals were killed here from 1786, when the islands were discovered by **PRO-MYSHLENNIKI,** to 1911, when an international agreement halted all hunting. **ALEUT** residents of the islands are now permitted to harvest a limited number of seals from St. Paul Island. St. George Island also has the largest seabird colony in the northern hemisphere, attracting about 2.5 million birds each summer. About 3,000 acres of their nesting area is included in the Alaska Maritime National **WILDLIFE REFUGE.**

PRINCE WILLIAM SOUND — **SOUND** off the Gulf of Alaska in **SOUTHCENTRAL** Alaska that is a mecca for commercial herring and **SALMON** fishermen, is traveled by the **STATE FERRY** that serves **WHITTIER, VALDEZ** and **CORDOVA,** and is

PRESERVATIONIST

also traveled by tankers on their way to and from the oil terminus at Valdez; also a popular sailing area.

PROMYSHLENNIKI (pro mish len' i kee) — Russian fur hunters and trappers who came to Alaska in droves in the late 1700s to kill sea otters, seals, foxes and other fur-bearing animals, and in the process decimated and enslaved the aboriginal **ALEUT** population. They were eventually brought under the command of the **RUSSIAN-AMERICA COMPANY**, which, with the influence of the **RUSSIAN ORTHODOX CHURCH**, curtailed their most barbarous acts. Many married **NATIVE** women and left their names and their genes as a legacy to many modern-day Alaskan families.

PROVE UP — To clear land and build the dwelling, often just a rough cabin, required for completing a **HOMESTEAD** application. Because of the effort and expense involved in bringing wilderness into agricultural production, some homesteads never got beyond the prove-up stage of development. See also **SWEAT EQUITY**.

PRUDHOE (proo' do) BAY — **NORTH SLOPE** location of the largest oil find in the history of Alaska and the northern hemisphere; subject of the 1969 $900 million oil lease sale; northern terminus of the **TRANS-ALASKA PIPELINE**; located along the northern coast of Alaska, along the **BEAUFORT SEA**, a little more than mid-way between **BARROW** and the Canadian border.

PTARMIGAN (tar' mi guhn) — Grouse-like bird that frequents the **TUNDRA** and willow flats across the state; changes color with the seasons, being brown or brownish-red in the summer and white in the winter. Prized as a game bird, it is said to be so tame and abundant at times it can easily be killed with a stick. Alaska has three different types: rock, white-tailed, and willow. The willow ptarmigan is Alaska's state bird.

PTARMIGAN

PUFFIN — Colorful, broad-beaked bird that nests in underground burrows and spends the rest of its time at sea. On land it looks like a small caricature of a real bird and on the sea it looks like a decorative fish float. Alaska has two varieties: horned and tufted. Both have orange beak tips, but the tufted is distinguished by long yellowish tufts of feathers that flow back from either side of its head. Also called sea parrot.

PURSE SEINE (pers' sayn') — Floating net that can be closed at the bottom, trapping **SALMON** within its confines; used by commercial **SEINERS**.

PUSHKI (poosh' kee) — Russian name commonly used for a large-leafed plant that has a single stalk topped by a parasol-shaped cluster of white flowers that grows throughout much of Alaska, from **SOUTHEAST** to the **SEWARD** Peninsula; also called wild celery and cow parsnip. **SUBSISTENCE** gatherers sometimes eat the tender young shoots or the roots of the plant and also use it for various medicinal purposes. Should not be confused with a somewhat similar, but quite deadly, plant, the poison water hemlock.

Q

QIVIUT (kiv' ee uht) — The soft underhair of the **MUSK OX** that is shed annually; the incredibly soft and fine yarn made from musk ox underhair that is knitted into scarves and hats and other clothing items and marketed exclusively by the **NATIVE** cooperative Oomingnak, also called the Musk Ox Producers Cooperative. Only Natives are allowed to sell this commodity, but anyone may buy it.

R

RAILBELT — The area from **SEWARD** to **FAIRBANKS** that is served by and borders the Alaska Railroad system. It comprises the most populous area in the state, incorporating Alaska's two largest cities, **ANCHORAGE** and Fairbanks, and the fast-growing Matanuska-Susitna **BOROUGH**.

RAVEN (ray' vuhn) — (1) Large, black, crow-like bird whose intelligence and apparently indomitable spirit has won it a place in **NATIVE** mythology throughout Alaska, where it is known as a trickster as well as a bringer of good things to humans, and occasionally as creator of the world; (2) one of the major **CLAN** divisions of the **TLINGITS** and **HAIDAS** of **SOUTHEAST** Alaska. Apparently impervious to bad weather, the raven can be found on the coldest and windiest days soaring above bluffs and hill tops, squawking and playing tag with its fellows.

RAZOR CLAMS — One of Alaska's favorite bivalves, gathered in summer by the hundreds by residents and tourists, from beaches along the **KENAI PENINSULA** and other coastal areas. Going for razors can be a challenge or a delight, depending on one's point of view. Since they often rest several inches below the surface and can burrow even deeper at the rate of nine inches a minute, they can take a lot of digging and a vigorous tug-of-war to unearth. In areas where they are heavily hunted, they may be only three or four inches long, but where they are allowed to mature, may reach lengths of eight to 10 inches. Oblong in shape, with dark brown or brownish-black shells, they resemble a wallet or a closed straight razor, which may account for the name. See also **CLAM**.

REDOUBT (ree' dowt) — (1) Russian fortress used during fur hunting and trading times, also called an "artel"; (2) 10,197-foot-high active volcano in the Chigmit Mountains on the west side of **COOK INLET** in **SOUTHCENTRAL** Alaska and within Lake Clark National Park, one of two perennially snow-clad mountains

RAZOR CLAM

that dominate the western skyline when viewed from the Sterling Highway on the **KENAI PENINSULA** south of **SOLDOTNA**.

REDS — Short, plural name for red **SALMON**, otherwise known as **SOCKEYE** salmon; called reds becaue they turn bright red in fresh water during **SPAWNING**.

REFUGE — Shortened version of National **WILDLIFE REFUGE**, land set aside by Congress and maintained for the protection of various animal species. The name is somewhat of a misnomer, since hunting and trapping are often allowed within refuge boundaries.

REGIONAL CORPORATION — NATIVE CORPORATION formed under the **ALASKA NATIVE CLAIMS SETTLEMENT ACT** to manage the money distributed under the act and control the economic development of land selected under it. There are 13 regional corporations within Alaska and one outside the state, which was organized for **NATIVES** who live elsewhere. The regional corporations also oversee the 203 Native village corporations.

REINDEER (rayn' deer) — Imported member of the deer family that is similar to the native **CARIBOU**; brought to Northwest Alaska in the 1890s to supplant dwindling food sources caused by overhunting of walrus and seal by American whalers; restricted to **NATIVE** herding and marketing; most commonly found in stores as reindeer sausage but most valuable for its horns, which are sold in the Orient for folk medicine and aphrodisiacs.

RICHARDSON, FORT — U.S. Army Base in **SOUTHCENTRAL** Alaska adjacent to **ANCHORAGE**, constructed in 1940 as part of the World War II build-up of Alaska's military defense system.

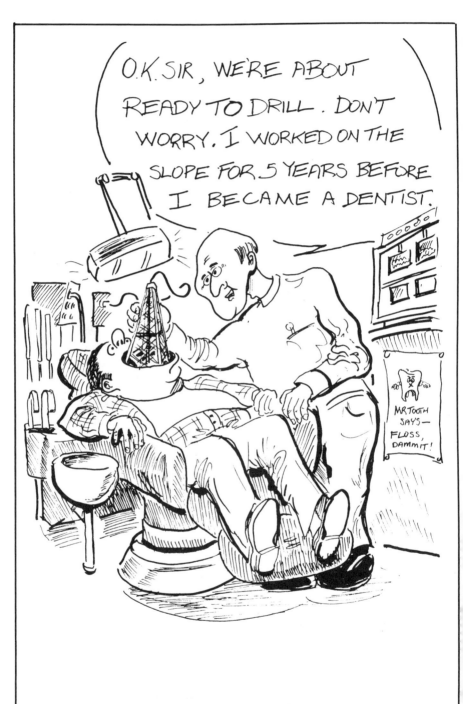

RIG

RIDGE — (1) Elevation of land with a long, relatively narrow crest; (2) elongated area of uplifted ice caused by the shifting of **PACK ICE** against itself or against the shore, called a pressure ridge.

RIG — (1) Short version of **DRILLING RIG**; (2) gear or equipment; (3) as a verb, to fit out with gear or equipment.

ROADHOUSE — Tavern or inn that serves as a way station along Alaska's highways and roadways; the earliest Alaska motels. Often located in isolated areas, roadhouses, which provided a warm bed and a meal, gave early travelers in the state something to look forward to and a welcome respite from the cold and the rigors of travel. Originally they were spaced about a day's journey apart and later they were spaced a gas fill-up apart.

ROCKER — Cradle used in **PLACER MINING** to separate gold from dirt and gravel. Earth was shoveled into the rocker, water poured on, and the cradle rocked; the gold was trapped by riffles built into the device and the rest of the material was washed away.

ROE (ro) — Fish eggs. Herring in Alaska are harvested primarily for their roe; **SALMON** roe is sometimes harvested for hatcheries, and sometimes packed up and sent to Japan as a delicacy. Caviar is preserved and salted roe.

RONDY — Shortest name for **ANCHORAGE**'s mid-winter fesival, the **FUR RENDEZVOUS**.

ROOKERY — Breeding place of sea birds or seals.

ROUGHNECK — Laborer on a **DRILLING RIG**.

ROADHOUSE₂: HOUSE ON A ROAD.

RUSSIAN-AMERICA COMPANY — Trading company that in 1799 got a monopoly license from Imperial Russia to gather furs, expand the empire and convert the NATIVES in Alaska. It claimed most of Alaska's coastline for Mother Russia, established an outpost at Fort Ross in Northern California, and even tried to establish a base in Hawaii. Many of Alaska's Natives still practice the RUSSIAN ORTHODOX faith and many bear the names left them by Russian hunters. The company sold its assets and closed its Alaskan bases when Russia sold Alaska to the United States in 1867 for $7.2 million. See also BARANOF, SHELIKOF, and ALASKA DAY.

RUSSIAN ORTHODOX CHURCH — First Christian church in Alaska and the one still followed by most of the NATIVES of Southwestern, SOUTHCENTRAL, and SOUTHEAST Alaska. Its missionaries stopped the most brutal practices of the PROMYSHLENNIKI, and educated as well as converted the Natives. The distinctive ONION DOME of its churches is a dominant feature of the skyline of many coastal villages. See also VENIAMINOF.

RUSSIAN VILLAGE — Generic name for the village of NIKOLAEVSK or any of the other villages on the KENAI PENINSULA inhabited by the OLD BELIEVERS. Other villages include Kachemak Silo, Razdolna, Dolena, and Vosnesenka.

S

SALMON (sam' uhn) — Backbone of Alaska's commercial fishing industry, which harvests tens of millions of salmon yearly, and annual quarry of thousands of sports anglers as well. Alaska's species include **KINGS** or **CHINOOKS**, **REDS** or **SOCKEYE**, **SILVERS** or **COHOES**, **PINKS** or **HUMPIES**, **CHUMS** or **DOG SALMON**. All are spawned and born in fresh water, migrate to sea as juveniles where they stay until they reach adulthood, and then return to the waters of their youth to spawn. Soon after **SPAWN-ING**, the fish die and riversides become littered with rotting carcases. Alive or dead, the salmon attract the attention of hungry **BEARS**.

SALTERY, SALTRY (sahl' tree) — Fish processing plant in the early days of Alaska's commercial fishing industry; used primarily for **SALMON** and herring, which were preserved by layering them with salt in huge barrels that weighed from 226 to 825 pounds.

SANDHILL CRANE — Large migratory bird that signals the changing of the seasons in many parts of Alaska. Its loud and distinctive cry, which seems an echo of prehistoric times, ushers in both spring and fall. About four feet tall, with a wingspan of nearly six and a half feet, it walks with stately grace and flies with amazing beauty. It is most spectacular when massing for migration, swirling overhead in large spirals to gain altitude.

SCRIMSHAW (skrim' shaw) — The art of carving or engraving designs on ivory and coloring the scored lines with some kind of ink or dye; most often associated with American whalers who developed the art form, perhaps emulating Oriental or **ESKIMO** artifacts seen during their travels, while passing the time between whales; now practiced by **NATIVES** and other artists and found in galleries and gift stores throughout the state. The only naturally occurring ivory in Alaska is walrus tusk, which, according to the **MARINE MAMMAL** Protection Act, can be collected and sold only by Natives. Most scrimshaw sold is either imported or fossilized ivory, which can be collected by non-Natives from private land or from public land with state or federal permission.

SEINER (say' ner) — Commercial fishing boat or enterprise

that goes after **SALMON** on the open water with a **PURSE SEINE**, surrounding the fish with the net and then closing the bottom and hauling it toward the boat where it can be emptied. Not to be confused with a **DRIFTER** or **SET NETTER**, which use nets that hang in the water like a sheet and entangle salmon in the mesh as they try to swim through. Seiners account for the vast majority of pink salmon and about half the overall commercial salmon catch in Alaska.

SELDOVIA (sel do' vee uh) — Small town on the south side of **KACHEMAK BAY** founded and still based on the commercial fishing industry; the name is Russian for "herring bay"; the major community on the western **KENAI PENINSULA** and freight depot for communities from Kasilof (kuh see' lawf) south until it was eclipsed by the city of **HOMER** in the late 1940s. It can be reached only by boat or plane.

SEISMIC (syz' mik) TRAIL — Swath cut through **TUNDRA, MUSKEG**, forest or field by companies exploring for oil or gas. Crews hoping to find underground geologic formations that indicate the possible presence of oil or gas set off small explosions at various points along the corridor that produce a graph of the subsurface formation. Seismic trails crisscross Alaska, sometimes lasting for decades after all exploration in the area has ceased.

SET — As a verb, to place nets in the water to trap fish; as a noun, the placement of the nets. Fishermen often talk about how many fish they harvested on one set.

SET NETTER — One who runs a commercial fishing operation from the beach by staking or anchoring gill nets into place and catching fish coming in on the tide; sometimes nets are laid out along the beach at low tide and then cleaned, or picked, of fish when the tide goes out again, but sometimes the nets are anchored in deep water and must be picked by boat (see **SKIFF**).

SEWARD (soo' urd) — (1)Coastal town of more than 2,000 people in **SOUTHCENTRAL** Alaska, at the head of Resurrection Bay on the east side of the **KENAI PENINSULA**; the terminus of the Alaska Railroad, and site of the annual Fourth of July **MOUNT MARATHON** run, a 3,022-foot uphill race; (2) peninsula in Northwestern Alaska, bordered by Norton **SOUND**, **KOTZEBUE** Sound, and the **BERING** Sea. Named for (3) William Henry Seward, American Secretary of State who negotiated the purchase of Alaska from Russia for $7.2 million in 1867 (see **ALASKA DAY**).

SEWARD'S DAY — Bank and civic holiday that commemorates the U.S. purchase of Alaska from Russia, recognized annually on the last Monday in March and celebrated by those who get the day off.

SHAMAN (shah' muhn, shay' muhn, or sham'uhn) — The religious leader and medical/ miracle worker of Alaska's aboriginal **NATIVE** cultures, an intensely powerful and important individual in tribal life who formed a living bridge between the natural and the spirit world, ultimately undermined and eventually supplanted by Christian missionaries and federal health workers.

SHELIKOF (shel' i kawf or shel' i kawv) — Also spelled Shelikov, Shelekhov, Shelikhov, Shelikoff, Shelikhof; (1) Grigorii, founder of the Shelikof-Golikhov Company that eventually became the **RUSSIAN-AMERICA COMPANY**, and the man who established the first Russian settlement in Alaska at Three Saints Bay on **KODIAK** Island; (2) strait between Kodiak Island and the Alaska **PENINSULA**.

SHOE PACS — Felt boots that fit inside rubber or leather boots to keep feet warm in the winter, occasionally worn around cabins in lieu of slippers; also used as a generic name for boots that have rubber feet and leather uppers and are lined with felt booties. See **SORELS**.

SILVERS — Silver SALMON, also known as COHO salmon, a 6 - 12 pound fighter that is one of Alaska's most popular sport fishing catches and serves as impetus for a number of salmon fishing derbies around the state; also popular with commercial fishermen, accounting for about 3 percent of the total commercial catch of salmon, and usually sold fresh, frozen or canned. The record is 26 pounds.

SITKA (sit' kuh) — Community of about 8,000 people on BARANOF Island in SOUTHEAST Alaska, southwest of JUNEAU; second capital of RUSSIAN AMERICA and original capital of Alaska; site of the transfer of Alaska to American hands; location of SHELDON JACKSON College and the Sitka Summer Festival of Music, which attracts musicians from all over the nation and around the world. It was originally a TLINGIT village, but when the Russians retaliated for the destruction of their Fort St. Michael in 1802 they drove the Indians off and appropriated the site.

SIX-PACK — (1) Small charter fishing boat licensed to carry up to six passengers; (2) quantity of beverage sometimes taken along by charter passengers or consumed after their return to port to celebrate the catch.

SIWASH (sy' wash) — (1) Derogatory name used by early prospectors and sailors to refer to Alaskan and Canadian Indians, now found only in the writings of the times or those that seek to recreate the period; (2) as a verb, to camp out with a tarpaulin or blanket in the open, or under a tree or some kind of crude shelter.

SKAGWAY — Boom town that sprang up at the head of the Lynn Canal in SOUTHEAST Alaska during the KLONDIKE GOLD RUSH of 1897, starting point for thousands of men and women headed for the CHILKOOT TRAIL, and prowling ground for SOAPY SMITH; now a town of about 1,000 people, who each year recreate the frontier days for hundreds of summer tourists who come to enjoy both the history and the beauty of the area;

southern terminus for Canada's White Pass Highway and for its now-discontinued Yukon and White Pass Railroad.

SKATES — (1) Bladed boots people put on their feet to help them move around on frozen lakes and ponds; (2) strings of fishing lines and hooks used by commercial **HALIBUT** fishermen; (3) edible flat fish, also called rays and manta rays, that hover just above the ocean floor and occasionally find their way to fish markets and the dining table.

SKIFF — Small boat used for fishing; **SEINERS** use them to pull the net to make a **SET**, **SET NETTERS** use them to set and retrieve nets, and sports fishermen use them to get out to where they hope the fish are biting.

SKILAK (skee' lak) — Approximately 12-mile-long lake on the **KENAI PENINSULA** in **SOUTHCENTRAL** Alaska, east of **SOLDOTNA.**

SKOOKUM (skoo' kuhm) — Native word adopted by **SOUR-DOUGHS** and other Alaskans meaning, depending on the context, strong, brave, hardy and game; often used to express admiration for a person or animal.

SLED DOG — Generally refers to **MALEMUTE** or **HUSKY**, but may be used generically to refer to any type of dog used to haul sleds.

SLEEPING LADY — Mount **SUSITNA**, a 4,396-foot-high mountain in **SOUTHCENTRAL** Alaska across **COOK INLET** from **ANCHORAGE**, so named because its configuration resembles a reclining figure.

SLIME LINE — The fish-cleaning assembly line in a **CAN-NERY.**

SLIP — Parking stall for boats in a harbor; what one is likely to do in winter without **ICE CREEPERS**.

SLOPE — (1) As a noun, the short name for the **NORTH SLOPE**, location of Alaska's largest oil find; (2) as an adjective, as in Slope coat or Slope worker, a reference to somebody or something associated with North Slope development.

SLUICE (sloos) BOX — Inclined wooden trough used in **PLACER MINING** to separate gold from gravel by washing the gravel off with a stream of water. See also **ROCKER**.

SNAG — To try to catch fish by hooking them through dorsal fins or other parts of their body, resorted to, usually illegally, when the fish aren't biting but the urge to catch a fish is.

SNOW BIRD — Seasonal worker who comes north for the summer and then takes his or her earnings south to warmer climes in the winter.

SNOW BLINDNESS — Temporary blindness caused by the glare of sun on snow or ice. Early **ESKIMOS** avoided it by wearing goggles of wood or bone with a narrow slit for the eyeholes; today people avoid it by wearing tinted sunglasses.

SNOW CRAB — **TANNER CRAB**, one of Alaska's commercial species, smaller in size but more plentiful than the **KING** crab, and larger than the Dungeness crab; harvested primarily in the **BERING** Sea and northern Gulf of Alaska; also called spider or queen crab.

SNOW-GO — Alternate name for snowmachine.

SLIP

SNOWSHOE — (1) Footgear resembling an elongated tennis racket without the handle, developed by the **ATHABASKANS** and adopted by other **NATIVE** groups, prospectors, and others for walking through deep snow (see also **BEAR PAWS**); (2) brown-in-summer, white-in-winter hare that populates most of Alaska and feeds lynx, owls, coyotes and other predators whose populations rise and fall with that of the hare, so called for its large, well-furred hind feet, which enable it to travel easily over the deepest and softest snow.

SOAKER (so' ker) — Extremely large **HALIBUT**; also called a **BARN DOOR**.

SOAPY SMITH — Chiseler, con-man, and petty gang leader who dominated **SKAGWAY**'s lawless early days, preying on miners and would-be prospectors on their way through town during the **KLONDIKE GOLD RUSH** and whose checkered career ended spectacularly in a waterfront shootout. He got his nickname through a con game in which he sold wrapped bars of soap to the gullible for exorbitant prices under the guise that some of the wrappings hid big money prizes. The only people ever to find money under the wrapper were his shills.

SOCKED IN — Prevented by bad weather or fog from traveling; **WEATHERED IN**.

SOCKEYE (sahk' y) — Alaska's second most plentiful **SALMON** species, also called red salmon or **REDS**; much prized for its firm red flesh, it is caught by the tens of millions each year and usually marketed frozen or canned, although there is a small but growing market for fresh packed reds.

SOLDOTNA (sahl daht' nuh) — City of about 3,600 people on the **KENAI PENINSULA** and seat of its **BOROUGH** government; founded, in the late 1930s or early 1940s, on agriculture but expanded due to the discovery of oil in surrounding areas; now dependent on oil, government, commercial fishing and tourism for its economic well-being. With its sister city **KENAI** and surrounding communities, it forms the population center of the peninsula. The name comes from the **DENA'INA** word "tsaldatnu," which means "trickles down creek" and originally referred to Soldotna Creek.

SOLSTICE — Twice yearly phenomenon that's shared by the rest of the world but especially appreciated in the far north, where the comings and goings of the sun have great significance. Winter solstice, marked elsewhere in the northern hemisphere as the beginning of winter, is celebrated in Alaska as the beginning of the end of the long night; at that point the days are as short as they get and from then until summer they just keep getting longer. Summer solstice marks the longest day of the year and is celebrated throughout the state by parties, picnics and all-night vigils. The length of the longest and shortest days varies according to the location in the state; the farther north one is, the longer the longest day, and the longer the longest night as well (see **BARROW**).

SORELS (suh relz') — Required footwear in much of Alaska, both in winter and in summer, popular because its rubberized foot keeps the wearer's feet dry under all sorts of adverse conditions and because its optional **SHOE PAC** keeps feet toasty warm in the frostiest weather. See also **BUNNY BOOT**.

SOUND — (1)Large arm of the sea, such as Norton Sound and **KOTZEBUE** Sound in Northwest Alaska and **PRINCE WILLIAM SOUND** in **SOUTHCENTRAL** Alaska; (2) as a verb, to dive, specifically referring to whales.

SOURDOUGH (sow' er do) — (1) A yeast-flour-and-water concoction made, preserved, carried, and treasured by Alaska pioneers and prospectors, who needed it to make bread, hotcakes, cake and other baked goodies, and who kept it alive by "feeding" it frequently with more flour and water or milk and making sure it didn't freeze or dry out; continuing mainstay of many Alaskan kitchens; (2) originally a prospector, now any old-time Alaskan, but particularly one who has spent a lot of time out in the **BUSH**.

SOUTHCENTRAL — Middle Alaska; the portion of the state that lies north of the Gulf of Alaska, south of **DENALI** National Park, east of **BRISTOL BAY** and west of **CORDOVA**; location of **ANCHORAGE**, the **KENAI PENINSULA**, the **MATANUSKA** Valley, and **CHUGACH** National Forest; population center of the state.

SOUTHEAST — The **PANHANDLE**; the **BANANA BELT** of Alaska; the thin section of Alaska that hugs the coastline between the Pacific Ocean and Canada; location of the **INSIDE PASSAGE**, **TONGASS** National forest, the state capital, and the state's largest concentration of bald eagles; home to the **TLINGIT**, **TSIMPSHIAN** and **HAIDA** Indians.

SOVEREIGNTY (sahv' ruhn tee) — Independent status sought by certain **NATIVE** groups that want to be viewed as tribal nations rather than American citizens, and want the special recognition and treatment that goes along with that designation; a source of controversy between various Native groups. Opponents see it as a way of losing what Natives have gained over the years; proponents see it as a way to assure Native rights and autonomy and protect their culture.

SOW — Female **BEAR**. Males are **BOARS** and offspring are **CUBS**.

SPAWNING — Natural fish reproduction. From summer to fall a succession of species of Pacific **SALMON** struggle up most of Alaska's rivers and streams to reproduce, after which they die. Females dig a depression, called a redd, in the streambed with their tails, lay their eggs, called **ROE**, and males cover the eggs with sperm, called milt. The hatchlings are called **FRY**, and while still small swim out to sea, where they spend one to six years growing to adulthood. Then they return to their home streams and repeat the reproductive process. Atlantic salmon do not die after spawning, but swim back out to sea. Fish **HATCHERIES** duplicate the reproduction process manually and release the fry in specific areas for later harvest.

SPENARD (spuh nahrd) DIVORCE — Spouse-icide, the quick and dirty but legally and ethically incorrect way to end a marriage and rid oneself of a mate by doing them in, occasionally the result of untreated **CABIN FEVER**; nearly made extinct by criminal prosecution, the 30-day divorce, and a plentitude of airline flights to sunny climes.

SPILL — Short term for oil spill, whether on land or sea and whether caused by the extraction or transportation of oil. Fear of pollution from spills led **CONSERVATIONISTS** and **PRESERVA-TIONISTS** to oppose the **TRANS-ALASKA PIPELINE** and the oil terminal at **VALDEZ**.

SPIT — Narrow finger of land extending into a body of water. **HOMER**, on **KACHEMAK BAY** in **SOUTHCENTRAL** Alaska, reputedly has one of the longest spits in the world, at four and a half miles.

SPOTTER — Airplane pilot who uses his aircraft to search for and spot schools of herring for commercial fishermen.

SPRUCE HEN — Spruce grouse, a chicken-size bird that frequents the forests of Alaska, but that can often be seen on dirt roads, picking up gravel to grind its food; one of four species of grouse that inhabit Alaska. Males are recognized by their bright red eye combs, which look like fiery Groucho Marx eyebrows. Although they can fly, most often they're seen on the ground.

SPENARD DIVORCE

SQUAW (skwaw) CANDY — Hard and chewy, dried or smoked **SALMON** that resembles jerky in texture; relished as a snack by people and dogs.

STARRING — The practice of carrying a star from house to house during Christmas celebrations in **RUSSIAN ORTHODOX** villages. It is accompanied by songs, prayers, and feasting and is one of the highlights of the season for believers.

STACK ROBBER — A device that rechannels heat that would otherwise rise up and out the chimney back into the room that's being heated.

STARTER — Wad of **SOURDOUGH** kept from each batch and used to start the next batch, the key to sourdough culture; to get it going, you mix in a little fresh flour and water, put it in a warm place, and let set overnight.

STATE FERRY — Common name for the Alaska **MARINE HIGHWAY** System and any of its vessels.

STATEHOOD — When Alaska became a state rather than just a territory of the United States; on Jan. 3, 1959, Alaska became the 49th state in the union.

STATE TROOPERS — Alaska's state police, responsible for enforcing laws everywhere in the state except in incorporated municipalities that have their own police forces.

STEAMERS — Little-neck clams, gathered with clam rakes or forks, and boiled or steamed or chopped up and used in clam chowder.

STEELHEAD — Sea-run rainbow trout popular with sports

fishermen for its fight and tasty flesh. It is a migratory fish that spends part of its time at sea and then returns to fresh water, where it becomes the prey of dozens of autumn anglers. The largest caught in Alaska weighed more than 42 pounds.

STELLER, GEORG — Naturalist with the **BERING** expedition of 1741-42; first European to realize Alaska was part of North America, indicated by the presence of a bird native to that continent, the Steller's jay, subsequently named for him. Other animals named for him are the Steller's sea lion and Steller's eider. He also authored the first ethnographic description of Alaska **NATIVES** on Kayak Island.

STIKINE (stik een') — Large, glacial river in **SOUTHEAST** Alaska, north of **WRANGELL**; waterway to the Canadian interior for the fur trade in the mid- to late-1800s and for gold hunters in the 1890s.

SUBSISTENCE (suhb sis' tens) — Hand-to-mouth living off the land by hunting, fishing, gathering, and sometimes growing what one eats; providing for one's provenance by one's own hand; a controversial issue that often pits **NATIVES** and the federal government against other Alaskans and the state Department of **FISH AND GAME**. The State Constitution gives subsistence a higher priority than any other type of harvesting, and the issue is whether Natives, because of their tradition and regardless of their income, have an inherent preferential right to the fish and game of Alaska over and above the rights of other Alaskans, including those with little or no income. The state has tried to mitigate the controversy by creating a **PERSONAL USE** fishery open to all Alaskans regardless of race or income, but that has not satisfied the federal government, which withheld management of Alaskan **MARINE MAMMALS** when the state sought it because it did not feel Native subsistence traditions were sufficiently protected under state law.

SUBSURFACE RIGHTS — Ownership of what is below the

MR. STELLER, THOUGH A GIFTED SCIENTIST, WAS NOT THE MOST POPULAR MAN ABOARD.

ground, i.e., oil and gas or other minerals; some early **HOMESTEADERS** got ownership of both what was above and below the ground they claimed, but most only got surface rights, with the state holding the right to exploit subsurface resources and liable only for surface damages.

SUNDOGS — Pseudo suns that occasionally appear on either side of the sun during the winter; mirror images of the sun caused by the reflection of sunlight off ice crystals in the air. The same phenomenon sometimes results in the appearance of a halo around the sun or moon.

SURIMI (suh ree' mee) — Fish paste made primarily from **BOTTOMFISH** and used to make imitation crab or shrimp or other types of exotic seafoods.

SUSITNA (soo sit' nuh) — River, valley, mountain, and small community in **SOUTHCENTRAL** Alaska adjacent to the **MATANUSKA** Valley. The river, which is a prime **SALMON SPAWNING** and popular fishing stream, was the focus of controversy in the mid-1980s because of a proposal to build a series of hydroelectric dams along its length. The project was ultimately scuttled because of cost and environmental concerns. The name is a **DENA'INA** Indian word meaning "sandy river," and was originally spelled "susitnu" or "suyitnu."

SWANSON RIVER — River on the **KENAI PENINSULA** in **SOUTHCENTRAL** Alaska; the area around it was the site of the first big oil discovery and drilling effort in Alaska, in 1957, which began a leasing boom and established oil development as a major industry in the state; site of a series of canoe trails.

SWEAT EQUITY — What **HOMESTEADERS** are said to have in the land they cleared and settled, gained through their own efforts rather than by monetary payment.

SWING DOG — Dog directly behind the **LEAD DOG** in a sled dog team.

T

TAIGA (ty' guh) — Northern coniferous forest of **INTERIOR** Alaska, named after the forests of eastern Russia; the word means "little sticks" and here refers to the spindly black spruce that dominate much of the forested area north of coastal Alaska, although the forest itself is often quite thick.

TALKEETNA (tahl keet' nuh) — (1) Small community in **SOUTHCENTRAL** Alaska, located along the **RAILBELT** north of **ANCHORAGE** near the **SUSITNA** River, that serves as a jumping off place for mountain climbing and flightseeing expeditions to Mount **McKINLEY**; (2) mountain range in Southcentral Alaska located northeast of **PALMER**. The town site was a former **ATHABASKAN** village that became a railroad work camp around 1916. The name has been said to mean either "river of plenty" or "where the rivers meet."

TANAINA (tuh ny' nuh) — Alternative spelling for the **DENA'INA** Indians that inhabited the coastal area near **COOK INLET** in **SOUTHCENTRAL** Alaska. They were **ATHABASKANS** but shared many of the cultural characteristics of their coastal neighbors, the **GULF COAST ESKIMOS**. They were the only Athabaskan Indian group to occupy a coast and combined coastal sea mammal hunting with inland hunting and fishing.

TANANA (ta' nuh naw) — (1)Valley that surrounds **FAIR-BANKS** and is the agricultural center for that area; (2) large river that flows northwest into **INTERIOR** Alaska from the Canadian border near the **ALCAN** and empties into the **YUKON** River; (3) Tanana Chiefs were a group of **ATHABASKAN** leaders that met with Congressional leaders in the 1900s and raised issues later settled by the **ALASKA NATIVE CLAIMS SETTLEMENT ACT**; (4) Tanana Chiefs Conference is one of the non-profit **REGIONAL NATIVE CORPORATIONS** established under the act. Tanana is an Indian word meaning "river trail."

TANNER CRAB — One of Alaska's three commercial species. Smaller than a **KING** crab and larger than a **DUNGIE**, it is prized for its long legs and sweet flesh, and provides the largest percentage of the commercial catch. More than 100 million pounds were harvested in 1986, out of a total shellfish catch of 148 million. It is also called **SNOW**, spider or queen crab.

TANNING — Turning animal skins from hides into leather, with or without the fur attached; requires treatment with tannic acid and lots of hard work. The **NATIVES** developed the process into a fine art, producing skins of incredible softness and durability.

TERMINATION DUST — Cold, white stuff that falls from the sky and signals the end of Alaska's all-too-short summer and the beginning of its frequently-too-long winter; a euphemism for snow, which isn't taken seriously in the fall until the weather is cold enough to keep it from melting; originally indicated the end of the construction and fishing season and the consequential termination of jobs; sign for **SNOW BIRDS** to head south.

THOUSAND MILE WAR — World War II campaign in the **ALEUTIAN ISLANDS** to drive out Japanese invaders. The war resulted in a military build-up across Alaska that created an economic boom for residents. See also **ATTU** and **KISKA**.

TIDAL FLAT — Another name for **MUD FLAT**, a flat area of sand or mud left high but not very dry at low tide and inundated at high tide; often characterized by sticky, gooey mud that can entrap the unwary or unwise who try to cross it.

TIDE BOOK — Book no sports or commercial fisherman, or smart beach hiker, should be without; it lists the times of daily high and low tides in the various coastal districts in the state. Available at **FISH AND GAME** offices and some sporting goods stores.

TIMBER — (1) Noun, trees or lumber; (2) verb, to buy drinks for everyone in the bar, initiated by the shout "timber" from a generous soul generally flush with either success or alcohol.

TIN CAN — Slang term for a metal, as opposed to a wooden, boat.

TLINGIT (tlin' kit, klink' it, tlin get') — Also spelled Tlinget, Thlingit, Thlinket; the largest **NATIVE** group in **SOUTHEAST** Alaska; in aboriginal times, Alaska's wealthiest and most aggressive Natives, who refused to be subjugated by the Russians and who kept them on uneasy footing by sporadic attacks as late as 1855; developers of the **CHILKAT** blanket and other distinctively stylized art forms; founders of the **ALASKA NATIVE BROTHERHOOD**; their forebears are believed to have arrived in Alaska from interior British Columbia 9,000 to 14,000 years ago.

TOE-PINCHING — Slang for trapping; refers to the capture of animals by their feet in steel traps and snares. Trapping has become a controversial issue in Alaska, with proponents saying it is a sport, tradition, and God-given right, and opponents saying it is an unspeakably cruel and indefensible act.

TOK (tok) — Community in eastern Alaska established in the

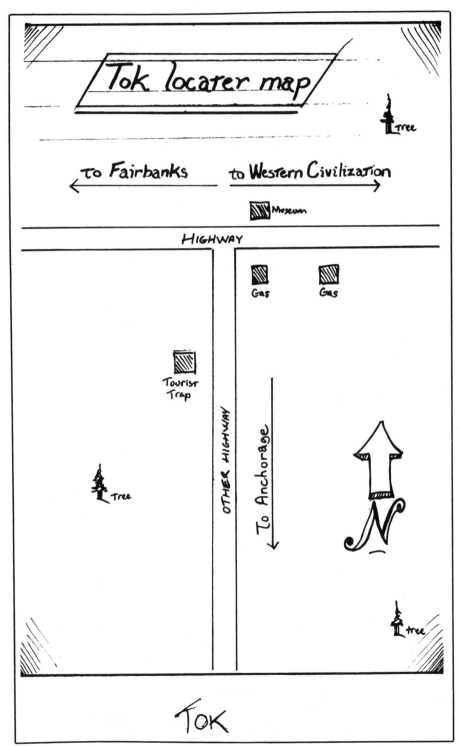

1940s during the building of the **ALCAN** and Glenn Highways; the first Alaska community drivers of the Alcan reach after they cross the Canadian border. The name is said to derive either from the Indian name for the nearby Tokai River, later changed to Tok, or from the Tokyo Camp of Alcan road builders.

TONGASS (tawn' guhs) — Nearly 17-million-acre national forest in **SOUTHEAST** Alaska, brought to the attention of the rest of the nation in the late 1960s, early 1970s and late 1980s by the controversy about the U.S. Forest Service's timber leasing policy and logging companies' **CLEAR-CUTTING** practices; the controversy surrounds ecological and aesthetic values versus economic values, and pits **CONSERVATIONISTS** against lumbermen, logging companies, and communities that are economically dependent upon the timber industry.

TOTEM (to' tuhm) — (1) Animal, plant or geographic feature taken as a symbol of a clan or tribal subdivision; (2) as in totem pole, a representation of animals and other beings having symbolic meaning to a particular individual, family, or **CLAN** of the **TLINGIT, HAIDA,** or **TSIMPSHIAN** and some **ATHABASKAN** Indians. Contrary to popular misconception, these were not idols and were never worshipped, but served much the same function as heraldry did in Europe.

TRANS-ALASKA PIPELINE — Pipeline constructed in the mid-1970s to carry crude oil from **PRUDHOE BAY** on the Beaufort Sea 800 miles south to the port of **VALDEZ**; most often called the **PIPELINE**.

TRAPLINE — Route along which traps are set to catch a variety of fur bearing animals; generally considered exclusive domain by the trapper, who checks it frequently to retrieve captured animals and reset traps; may range from several miles to over 100 miles in length. Originally traveled by dog sled, but now most often serviced by snowmachine.

TROLLING

TRAWL — To commercially fish for species that stay at the bottom of the ocean by dragging a bag-like net along the seabed; the net used for this type of fishing. Not to be confused with **TROLL**.

TROLL — To fish by pulling a baited hook or lure behind a slowly moving boat; some small-scale commercial fishermen in **SOUTHEAST** Alaska fish for salmon by trolling.

TSIMPSHIAN (sim' shee uhn) — Also spelled Tsimshian and Tsimpshean, the smallest and most recently-arrived **NATIVE** group in **SOUTHEAST** Alaska; moved to Annette Island from Canada in 1887 under the leadership of William Duncan, a Church of England missionary, after the U.S. Congress established a reservation for them there. They share many of the cultural characteristics of their neighbors, the **HAIDA** and **TLINGIT**. See **METLAKATLA**.

TSUNAMI (soo nah' mee) — Tidal wave; seismic sea wave caused by earthquakes, volcanic eruptions, or other oceanic disturbances of major proportion. Tsunamis created by the **GOOD FRIDAY EARTHQUAKE** of 1964 wiped out the original town of **VALDEZ** and the port of **SEWARD**, and left boats at **KODIAK** high and dry in the middle of town; since then Alaska has developed a tsunami warning system for its coastal communities.

TUNDRA (tuhn' druh) — Treeless expanse that covers much of Alaska and consists of a myriad of low-lying, dwarfed plants, mosses and lichen. **ARCTIC** tundra is low-lying, alpine tundra is above treeline.

TURNAGAIN (tern' uh guhn) — Arm of **COOK** Inlet south of **ANCHORAGE** that borders the northern end of the **KENAI PENINSULA**; called the Turnagain River by Capt. James Cook in 1778, after he was forced to turn back there in his search for the **NORTHWEST PASSAGE**.

PRECAUTIONS TAKEN IN COMMUNITIES
IN TSUNAMI RISK AREAS.

TUSTUMENA (tuhs tuh mee' nuh) — (1) 24-mile-long lake on the **KENAI PENINSULA** in **SOUTHCENTRAL** Alaska, named by the **DENA'INA** "Dustubena" or "peninsula lake"; (2) of of the **STATE FERRIES**, affectionately called by those it serves, the "Rusty Tusty."

TWO-FOOT HIGH KICK — Event in the **WORLD ESKIMO INDIAN OLYMPICS** where the contestant jumps into the air, kicking both feet in front in an attempt to hit a hanging seal skin ball; both feet must remain together from lift-off to set-down; the record is 8'1''. See also **ONE-FOOT HIGH KICK.**

TYONEK (ty on' ek) — **TANAINA** Indian community in **SOUTHCENTRAL** Alaska southwest of **ANCHORAGE**, on the western shore of **COOK INLET**. The **ATHABASKAN** word means "little chief"; the **ESKIMO** word for the area, "Tu i u nuk," means "marsh people."

U

ULU (oo' loo) — **ESKIMO** woman's knife, used for skinning, scraping, slicing, dicing, and for any other household need; originally made of stone with a bone handle, now most often made of metal and wood. Fan-shaped, it is held at the narrow end by a wooden handle laid across the flat of the palm of the hand. It comes in two sizes: a small one, used for sewing, and a larger one used for cutting meat or fish.

UMIAK (oo' mee ak) — Open, skin-covered boat with a

wooden frame, developed and used by the **ESKIMOs** for carrying groups of people, as opposed to the **KAYAK**, which carried only one or two, and used for whale hunting as well as for transportation.

V

VALDEZ (val deez') — Small coastal city of about 3,000 people in **SOUTHCENTRAL** Alaska on the northern shore of **PRINCE WILLIAM SOUND** that is the southern terminus for the **TRANS-ALASKA PIPELINE**; the old town, at the head of Valdez Arm, was established during the **GOLD RUSH** and was destroyed in 1964 by a **TSUNAMI** caused by the **GOOD FRIDAY EARTH-QUAKE**. The town's name, although considerably Americanized, is a legacy of Spanish explorations in Alaskan waters in the 18th century.

VENIAMINOV (ven yah' min awf) IVAN — Russian Orthodox religious leader who served in Alaska during the **RUSSIAN AMERICAN** period first as priest and missionary in the **ALEUTIAN ISLANDS** and then as Bishop Innocent of Alaska in **SITKA**. He eventually went on to hold his church's highest office, Archbishop or Metropolitan of Moscow. Revered by Russian and **NATIVE** alike, he was the first person to devise a grammar and dictionary of the **ALEUT** language and to describe the Aleut culture in detail.

VOLCANO — Mountain formed by the upwelling of molten rock through the earth's crust. Alaska has 57 volcanoes, 35 of them active, primarily along the **ALEUTIAN CHAIN**, the Alaska Peninsula, and the west shore of **COOK INLET**. Active volcanoes that can be seen from the highway in **SOUTHCENTRAL** Alaska include Mount Wrangell, Mount Torbert, Mount Spurr, **REDOUBT**, **ILIAMNA**, and Mount **AUGUSTINE**, which erupted last in 1986. The biggest Alaska eruption in modern history occurred in 1912 at Mount **KATMAI** and buried the town of **KODIAK**, 100 miles away, under 18 inches of ash.

W

WAINRIGHT — (1) Fort, U.S. Army base in **INTERIOR** Alaska near **FAIRBANKS**, activated in 1940 as Ladd Field, an Army Air Corps base, and transferred to Army jurisdiction in 1961; (2) **ESKIMO** village on the **ARCTIC** coast southwest of **BARROW**.

WASILLA (wah sil' uh) — Town of about 3,600 people in **SOUTHCENTRAL** Alaska west of **PALMER**; established in 1916 as a railroad station and named for a chief of the **KNIK** Indians; it has been speculated that the name is a derivation of the Russian name Vasiliev.

WEATHERED IN — Kept from traveling by bad weather; also called **SOCKED IN**.

WHEEL DOGS — Dogs harnessed directly in front of the sled in a dog sled team.

WHISKEY JACK — Nickname for the Canada Jay. See also **CAMP ROBBER**.

WHITE ALICE — Communications system developed by the

military in the late 1950s that relied on several huge, rectangular antennas to reflect radio signals; its name derived from Alaska Integrated Communications Extension; ultimately made obsolete by satellite technology, but the antennas can still be seen in some places.

WHITE KNUCKLE SPECIAL — Rough commuter airline flight, so-called because of the tendency of the passenger to grip the back of the seat in front until the knuckles turn white; characterized by shuddering, of both plane and passengers, wing dips and sudden stomach-churning drops in altitude. Should not be confused with the Red Eye Special, which is a middle of the night or very early morning flight and which may or may not also be a white knuckle special.

WHITE OUT — Winter weather condition in which driving snow obliterates all familiar objects and shapes and makes walking, driving, or flying a perilous adventure; a blizzard.

WHITE PASS — One of two passes that led from **SKAGWAY** to the goldfields of the **KLONDIKE**; ultimately the route of a railway between Skagway and Whitehorse, Yukon Territory, and a subsequent highway; the narrow-gauge railroad, built 1898-1900 and used until the early 1980s, cost $10 million to build and climbed 2,885 feet in 21 miles.

WHITE SOCKS — Irritating little biting flies that swarm and plague people during the summer months; so-called because their feet, when one can see them, are said to be white. They are a variety of black fly, of which there are over 30 species in Alaska.

WHITTIER — Port and railroad and **STATE FERRY** terminal on **PRINCE WILLIAM SOUND** in **SOUTHCENTRAL** Alaska; The

detail

WHITE OUT AT BETTLES, AK 1972

WHITE-OUT CONDITIONS

town, which now has a population of about 340, was built in World War II as an Army base, but the Army abandoned the base in 1960. Named for Whittier Glacier, which was named for the poet John Greenleaf Whittier in 1915.

WILDLIFE REFUGE — Short name for one of Alaska's 16 National Wildlife Refuges; federal preserve set aside for the overall protection of animals and their habitats. See **REFUGE**.

WILLIWAW (will' i waw) — Sudden strong gusts of wind that occasionally reach speeds up to 100 knots, or 115 miles, and are particularly prevalent in Alaska along the **ALEUTIAN** Chain.

WIND CHILL FACTOR — The effective temperature on windy days, determined by the relationship of temperature to wind speed. On a zero degree day with a wind of 10 miles an hour, the wind chill factor is minus-21 degrees Fahrenheit. Forty-mile-an-hour winds produce the same wind chill factor on a 20 degree day.

WOOLY MAMMOTH — The official state fossil of Alaska; extinct large, long-haired relatives of the elephant that roamed unglaciated areas in Alaska during the ice age. They became extinct 12,000 years ago but are occasionally found frozen in **PERMAFROST**.

WORLD ESKIMO INDIAN OLYMPICS — **NATIVE** sport competition held each year in July in **FAIRBANKS**; the events are tests of endurance, strength, and skill that derive from traditional Native culture.

WRANGELL (rang' guhl) — (1) Island and community of about 2,400 people in **SOUTHEAST** Alaska that began life as an Indian village, progressed to trading post for both the **RUSSIAN-AMERICA COMPANY** and the British, U.S. Army base, and jum-

WOOLY MAMMOTH   ACRYLIC MAMMOTH

ping off place for the Cassiar gold fields in British Columbia, and is now predominantly dependent on commercial fishing, logging and summer tourism; (2) mountain and mountain range in **SOUTHCENTRAL** Alaska, northeast of **CORDOVA** and **VALDEZ**, west of Glennallen, and south of **TOK**, that extends to the Canadian border and forms part of the 12-million-acre Wrangell-St. Elias National Park; all were named for (3) Baron Ferdinand Wrangell, sixth governor of Russian America, who served from 1830 to 1835 and encouraged increased exploration into western and **INTERIOR** Alaska.

XYZ

YAKUTAT (yak' uh tat) — Coastal community of about 500 people in **SOUTHEAST** Alaska, on the Gulf of Alaska, that came to national attention in 1986 because of its proximity to Hubbard **GLACIER**, which grew so rapidly it closed the mouth of a fjord and trapped numbers of seals and porpoises in the lake it thereby created; site of one of Russian America's first and least successful agricultural colonies, one that existed in fear, deprivation, hunger, sickness and strife from its inception in 1795 until its destruction by **TLINGIT** warriors in 1802.

YUKON (yoo' kahn) — (1) Canadian territory that shares a common border with Alaska, first known by Americans as the home of the **KLONDIKE GOLD RUSH** (would-be prospectors often said they were either going to the Klondike or to the Yukon); (2) 2,300-mile-long river that is both the longest and largest in Alaska, flowing from Canada, across **INTERIOR** Alaska, and emptying into the **BERING** Sea.